To FRANK
Best
Tom

Further Useful Tips for Woodcarvers

D0831678

Further Useful Tips for Woodcarvers

Guild of Master Craftsman Publications Ltd

This collection first published in 2000 by
Guild of Master Craftsman Publications Ltd,
Castle Place, 166 High Street, Lewes,
East Sussex BN7 1XU

Front cover photograph by John Beart (see 'Bean bag holder' on page 50)
Illustrations by Simon Rodway

ISBN 1 86108 147 2

A catalogue record of this book is available from the British Library

Designed by Edward Le Froy

Printed and bound in Great Britain
by Ebenezer Baylis & Son Ltd

Contents

Techniques

Clamps and workholders

Sanding and abrasives

Preparing and decorating wood

Introduction

THEY SAY necessity is the mother of invention, and this book of inspiring tips and ideas, gathered from the pages of *Woodcarving* magazine, is testament to that saying.

Solving problems and saving cash is the name of the game here. If there is an awkward piece of wood to be held, some special tool needed, or a more convenient way of working required, then you can guarantee that some resourceful woodcarver will come up with just the right solution – and the generosity of carvers is such that, if they have an ingenious idea or useful bit of information, then they will pass it on.

Some of these tips are completely new and some are old ideas improved or adapted, but all are designed to make life easier, and often cheaper, in the workshop. We can all learn something from each other, and I hope you will find many new ideas here to help you in your craft.

Nick Hough
Editor, *Woodcarving*

Equipment

TOOL TRAY

There are many small, freestanding carving benches with ball-and-socket-type work clamps available on the market these days, but not so many tool holders suitable to use with them.

I made my own adjustable and portable tool tray with some scrap blockboard, timber, casters and a metal shelving rack with brackets.

The base is a 510mm (20in) square blockboard with light casters fixed to each corner.

Braced lengths of 75 x 50mm (3 x 2in) timber are fixed above, with metal shelf holders screwed to each side.

This gives a platform on which to place tool trays to your individual requirements. Mine have recessed dividers to separate chisels, gouges, knives, pencils and a mallet.

It is useful when demonstrating to have your tools in their place at all times for safety and security.

The shelving system means the trays can be adjusted from about 1m (39in) high to suit a standing person, down to a height suitable for a seated carver without having to alter the basic tray's structure.

Clive Price

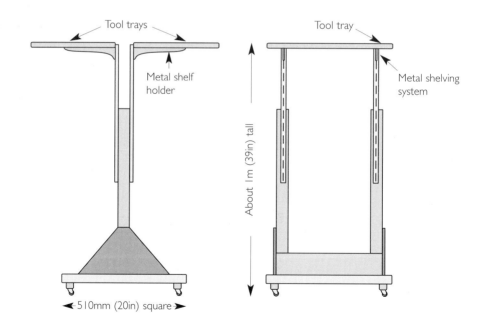

Tool tray, front and side views

TOOL CADDY

If, like me, you carve away from home and workshop sometimes, you need somewhere to keep your tools while working. It is inconvenient to take a table with you or to put the tools on the ground.

I carve sitting down in a folding chair, and I have made a wooden tool caddy which attaches to the chair arm with metal brackets.

The caddy is about 305 x 200 x 25mm (12 x 8 x 1in) deep. It keeps the tools safe and I can arrange them in order for easy retrieval.

You can line the tray with felt, cork or foam if you wish.

If you add a hinged lid and catch to the tray, you can use the tray to carry the tools as well.

R B Himes

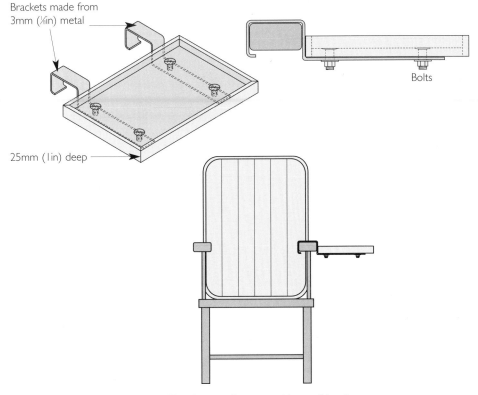

Brackets made from 3mm (⅛in) metal

Bolts

25mm (1in) deep

Tray fixes to chair arm with metal brackets

SIMPLE STORAGE

I carve lots of small items for sale at fairs and markets for charity and, as they have to be stored for some time, I need to keep them safe.

I store them in different-sized empty plastic ice cream containers, with lids, all clearly labelled on my shelf.

This protects them from damage, dust and cracks caused by drying out too quickly.

Patricia Vardigans

CHEAP CASE

As a member of the BWA I often take tools and carvings to exhibitions. This means making carrying cases, which can be expensive if you have to buy fittings such as catches, hinges and handles.

I find a cheap way is to use old leather belts bought for a few pence at jumble sales.

I cut a short piece off at the buckle end and another piece from the holes end to make catches. These are screwed to the body and lid of the case with round-headed screws.

Two more short pieces screwed across the back of the body and lid make hinges, and the rest of the belt makes a handle.

Ted Jeffery

STAND IT

Being both a carver and a musician, I find my old music stand is perfect for holding my drawings, photographs and plans so I can refer to them while I am carving.

It is fully adjustable and allows me to work 360° round my carving stand.

M Ninham

CLEAN FILES

We all suffer from wood-clogged files, particularly files with fine teeth used for final shaping. You can clean them with brushes, but not always easily or thoroughly.

As wood swells when wet, I tried putting my files in water. Within a few seconds the wood dust floated off and I had just to rub the files with my fingers for a few seconds.

Files must be fully dried to prevent rust, so it is best to use hot water, as this speeds the process and helps to dry the file afterwards.

Antoine Delsemme

CARVING BENCH TOOL HOLDER

This handy swing tool holder was made to use with my 'sit-astride carving bench' (see page 51).

I made the tool holder from a 420 x 165 x 20mm (16½ x 6½ x ¾in) piece of wood I rescued from a builder's skip. I cut out one corner to the shape shown, so I could rest my knee against it when it was swung out and in use.

I rounder and smoothed all edges of the wood, then drilled 13 holes 16mm (⅝in) diameter to hold my chisels. I wanted the top three holes to be larger to hold bigger octagonal handles and, as I do not have a larger bit, I made the holes bigger with a round surform blade.

Three other holes were made slightly larger to take brass ferrules, and one hole was made extra large for a wide gouge. All holes are marked to indicate which tools they hold.

I drilled a further hole near the neck of the tool holder to take a 75mm (3in) bolt which would secure the holder to the bench with a washer and nut.

I drilled the corresponding hole in a corner of the bench, placed so that I could use it either when I am sitting astride the bench with a carving clamp attached, or when I am sitting on the bench, carving on my lap.

Left-handed carvers could simply fix the holder on the other side.

Patricia Vardigans

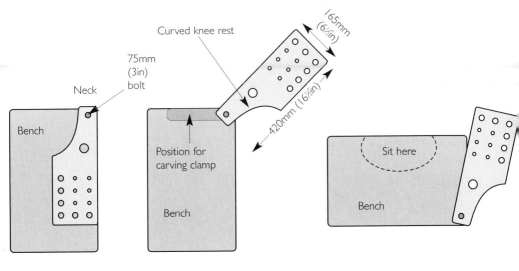

Top view of bench with tool holder in closed position for storage

Top view of bench with tool holder in open position ready for use

Top view of bench with tool holder positioned for use when lap carving

Easier Gluing

Once a plastic bottle of woodworking glue is nearly empty, it can be frustrating waiting for it to dribble out.

I now transfer the glue into one of the thin plastic bottles used for shampoo and shower gel, well washed out, of course.

I use the type with a large hook on the cap to enable the container to hang upside down.

The flip–top lid on mine is ideal for spreading and controlling the flow of adhesive, and the bottle hangs conveniently so there is no waiting, no mess and no stress.

Peter Griffiths

Shower gel or shampoo bottle for holding glue

Template Shapes

When doing plaque relief carvings I often use templates for getting an exact oval or round shape. To find the appropriate shape, I use items from the kitchen – plates, saucers, cups, soup bowls, mugs, oven dishes, flan tins, saucepan lids and so on.

If the outline is too big or small for my wood I trace the shape on to paper and use a photocopier to enlarge or reduce it to the size I need.

I then use carbon paper to transfer the shape on to card and cut round it to make my template.

By mixing different sizes and shapes together I can make further interesting outlines, saving time and money.

When I wanted to copy a twisted knot design from a photograph, I bought a 405mm (16in) flexible curve from an art shop and used this to copy the design on to paper.

The finished design was then carbon copied directly on to the wood and gave me several hours of enjoyable relief carving.

Patricia Vardigans

Bench support

Lots of carvers like me use a Black & Decker Workmate or similar type of workbench for woodcarving. Unfortunately I find this too low for carving in comfort, and I have also seen others bending awkwardly low over their work.

To remedy this I made a simple box frame of 50 x 50mm (2 x 2in) wood on which I can stand the bench.

I extend the Workmate's folding legs, and the box frame fits between them.

The frame is 330mm (13in) wide, the right size to fit between the bench legs, and 380mm (15in) high. There is also an extra 75mm (3in) section on each end of the frame, so it can be 380mm (15in) or 460mm (18in) high, depending on which way up it is placed.

The frame is 865mm (34in) long, so the Workmate can be slid along it while I am working to reach other parts of the carving.

Since using the frame I have had no more back trouble.

S Lord

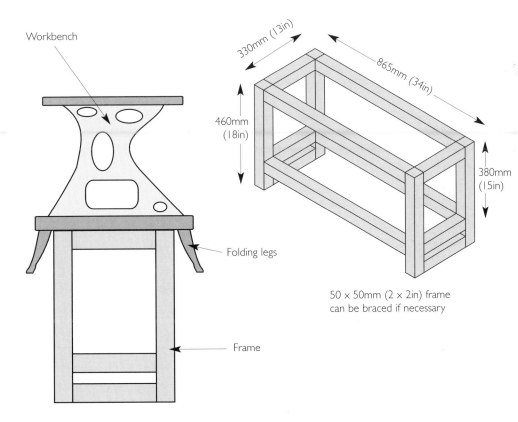

Workbench

330mm (13in)

865mm (34in)

460mm (18in)

380mm (15in)

Folding legs

50 x 50mm (2 x 2in) frame can be braced if necessary

Frame

Frame for workbench

DEPTH CUTTING JIG

I had a large amount of incised carving to do in ordinary soft wood, and I soon found it difficult to maintain a constant width of groove with a V tool.

To overcome this difficulty I made a depth stop from boxwood (*Buxus sempervirens*). This took the form of a sleeve, which was drilled to be a push fit over the V tool.

The sleeve was shaped as shown in the drawing and secured in position with a self tapping screw.

I found this worked well and, as a bonus, the pressure of the shoulders of the jig on the soft wood kept the edges of the groove from tearing out.

This should work equally well with a veiner gouge.

T J Austin

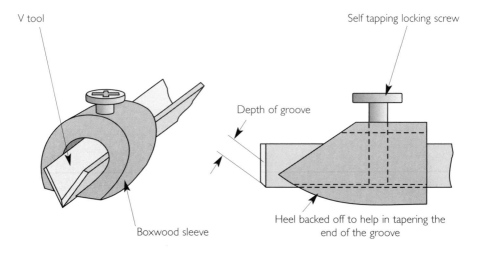

V tool

Self tapping locking screw

Depth of groove

Boxwood sleeve

Heel backed off to help in tapering the end of the groove

POWER TIPS

Here are a few ideas which I find useful when using various power tools.

Variable speed is essential for many jobs, yet speed controls are often difficult to obtain. I use an ordinary transformer, which reduces the voltage and therefore the speed.

Flexible drive tools lose much of their power in the flexible shaft, so it is more efficient to use a die grinder. If you do not have one, it is often possible to remove the base plate from a router, and use this with your carbide burrs.

If you use an engraving machine for embossing, punching and sandblasting effects, it is best to suspend the machine from the ceiling with rubber bands, making it almost weightless. This makes it easier for you to achieve precise control.

Rod Naylor

MEATY MALLETS

I have read of carvers, including Chris Pye, using metal mallets for woodcarving, but I feel there is an unacceptable and avoidable risk of damage to chisel handles by direct contact with unyielding metal.

I wanted the benefit of smaller sized mallets with greater weight than metal mallets would provide and the answer was to turn a wooden mallet 170mm (6¾in) long by 55mm (2¼in) wide at its widest part. I hollowed out the inside of the mallet head, leaving a wall or rim thickness of about 12mm (½in), and certainly no less than 10mm (⅜in).

I braced some nails across the recess to provide a key, then filled it with molten lead. **N.B. This needs to be done wearing protective clothing, and with great care, as splash burns are particularly nasty.**

This gave me a mallet of 1lb 6oz (624g) total weight.

The action of these mallets is excellent, much better than lignum vitae (*Guaiacum officinale*), and they do not damage chisel handles. Any size and weight of mallet can be made.

They are also cheap, as second-hand lead is inexpensive and you can use hardwood offcuts. I have used laburnum (*Laburnum anagyroides*), apple (*Malus pumila*), yew (*Taxus baccata*) and blackthorn (*Prunus spinosa*).

Geoffrey Thompson

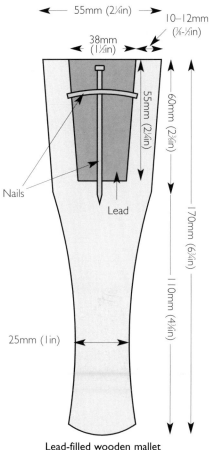

Lead-filled wooden mallet

WEIGHT LIFTING

Power tools such as die grinders and angle grinders are great for use with carving discs, but can be too heavy for use over prolonged periods. Working when tired risks accidents to the work or yourself.

My solution is to put a hook in my ceiling, from which I can suspend my power tools on a length of heavy elastic, such as a bungee cord or a bicycle inner tube.

For those with low ceilings in their workshops, a length or cord passing through two pulleys with a counter-balance weight on the end could be the answer.

Rod Naylor

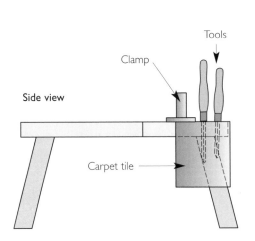

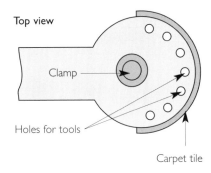

Side view

Clamp

Tools

Carpet tile

Top view

Clamp

Holes for tools

Carpet tile

SAFETY SCREEN

There must be many carvers who use a sit-on carving bench like mine, which has a series of holes drilled around the front end to take chisels and gouges.

This means that the blades of the tools point downwards towards the floor and, if you drop something and reach down to pick it off the floor, there is a danger you could accidentally catch your hand on one of the exposed blades.

They are also a potential hazard for children or pets who may get under the bench.

To prevent this danger, I fitted a foam-backed carpet tile round the front edge of the bench. I just cut the tile to the right size and glued and tacked it on. I have found this to be very effective.

W E Protheroe

BLOW IT!

For a recent commission of a rosette, the eyes of the foliage were small and deep and I found it difficult to clear the chips from inside.

I took a plastic straw, saved from a fast food restaurant, and used it like a pipette to blow out the recesses.

You have to be careful not to fill the hole up with fluid!

Fred Wilbur

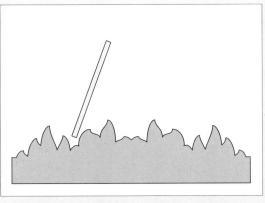

Straw used to blow wood chips from recesses

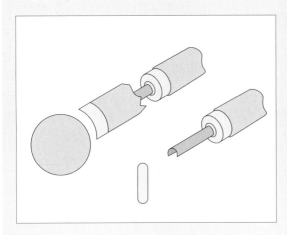

Template Aids

I find that having cardboard templates for each of my gouge profiles makes marking out much easier. The templates can be colour coded or numbered to identify each gouge, and they can be bent around curved work.

Another device I use is a piece of carpet to lay my tools on. This stops them jumping off the bench when I am thumping with a mallet.

Arthur Cross

Banish drips

When applying a finish such as varnish to a carving like a sign, it is difficult to stop drips running down the side and leaving ugly lumps underneath.

To overcome this problem, I made a stand, which enables me to wipe the underneath of the sign to get rid of all drips. It also allows air to circulate, helping drying.

The stand is simply a board 355 x 125mm (14 x 5in) with two rows of four staples knocked into it. I made sure they were level by turning the board over and using a spirit level.

When I turn the sign over to varnish the back I use small rubber walking stick ferrules to prevent dents or scratches.

Rachel Endacott

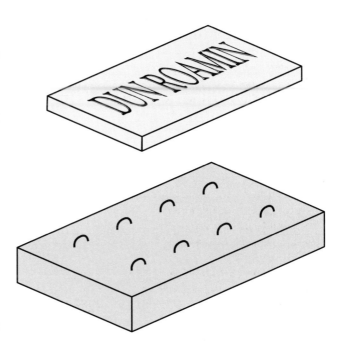

SCALING CARVINGS

If you want to scale up carvings, making or buying scaling callipers (inside and outside) and dividers can be expensive, especially when they are used only occasionally.

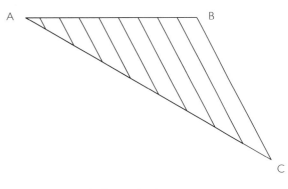

Instead I use ordinary callipers and this simple diagram.

The line A–B should represent the maximum size of your drawing, photograph, model or whatever.

The line A–C should equal the maximum size of the intended carving.

Scaling up drawing

Join line B–C before making a series of lines parallel to B–C.

Any measurement on the original drawing, photograph or model (line A–B) can then be picked off on line A–C to give an accurate scaled copy.

Rod Naylor

CHISEL HOLDER

I have made a board on a stand with holes of 20, 15 and 12mm (¼, ⅜ and ½in) to hold my chisels.

This keeps my tools handy, stops them rolling off the bench, and ensures the cutting edges are kept safely out of the way.

Derek Shuttler

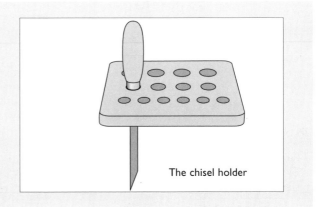

The chisel holder

AVOIDING CRAMP

When doing a series of repeat carvings with a 3mm (⅛in) No 15 parting tool, I held the tool close to its blade like a pencil, for control, but found this caused cramp in my fingers.

To overcome this I wrapped the shank of the tool with tape. This increased the circumference, which helped both with comfort and controllability of the tool.

Fred Wilbur

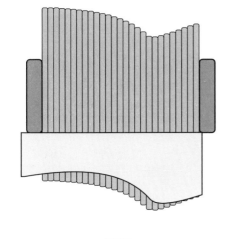

Left: the cardboard template shows the mismatch between the shape of the carved wood and the desired one

Below left: pressing the profile gauge on the carving to obtain its shape

Below: the template is placed on the profile gauge to show the mismatch. This can be drawn on the gauge and then transferred to the carving

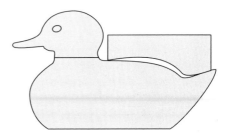

PERFECT PROFILES

As a novice carver I found I left my bird carvings with too square a cross-section.

To try to avoid this I made cardboard templates from a cross-sectional projection of my carving patterns, but still had problems because, when I laid the templates on the carvings, I found it difficult to establish exactly where the excess was and how much needed to be removed.

I have now reduced this problem considerably by using a DIY tool, a plastic profile gauge.

This has a set of plastic pins, which slide together and take up the profile of whatever they are pressed against. The gauge is normally used for cutting carpets or vinyl round architraves, and so on.

I now still use the template, but lay the profile gauge on the carving and, after setting in, place it and the template together so the position and degree of mismatch can be easily seen.

If necessary, this can be marked on the profile gauge with non-permanent felt tip pen. The gauge can then be carefully replaced on the carving, and the appropriate area shaded in pencil on the wood to show what needs to be removed.

Gerry Sanger

Tools

HANDY TOOLS

I have found two non-carving tools which help overcome problems with my relief carvings.

The first is a car tyre tread depth gauge which, used with a ruler or set square placed across the top of the wood, enables you to maintain accurate depths of cut across a carving of any size. I used this on a wall plaque, having first paced out the various reference points to aid my design, and to calculate the depths required for accurate perspective.

My second tool is an acetate transparency sheet as used on an overhead projector. On to this I photocopy or trace the carving design. With this I can maintain the outline I have just carved away and, at the same time, view the progress of work done by placing the acetate over the wood.

Alec Baxter

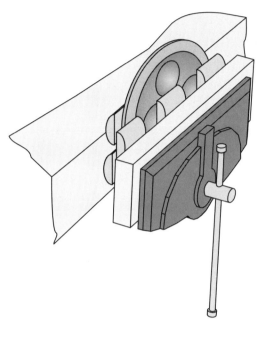

Using a tyre depth gauge on a relief carving

SHARP SHEARER

When I had difficulty carving a vertical face into a concave form I modified an old chisel into the shape shown in the illustration.

Since achieving success with this format, I have found treating the radius and angle as variables I can cope with any texture of wood.

Chris Brown

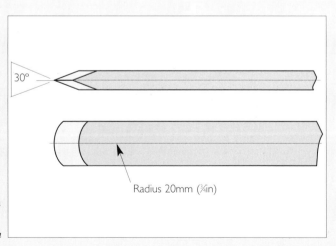

30°

Radius 20mm (¾in)

CHEAP DRAWKNIFE

I use a lot of green wood for my carvings, and one of the most useful tools I have is a small drawknife which I made using an old, broken, hacksaw blade.

I ground one edge of the blade to a 30° bevel, flattened the back of the edge on a honing stone and sharpened the bevel edge. I then stropped the blade to polish the cutting edge, and removed any grit, dirt or paint from the blade.

For handles I used curved plastic drawer handles. One end of the blade had a hole drilled in it, and I drilled another hole the other end, then screwed the handles on.

You can use any handles, wooden drawer knobs or turned handles if you wish.

You can cut either with the bevel up or down. As the blade is flexible it can follow contours of the wood, but the blade is brittle so do not flex it too far or it will break.

Graeme Vaughan

HAND TOOLS FROM OLD BLADES

High speed hacksaw blades are made from some of the finest steel available, capable of holding a very sharp edge, yet we regularly throw them away instead of making more tools from them.

The best blades are the thicker ones made for machine hacksaws (you cannot use bimetallic blades).

First grind off the worn teeth and strip any paint from the sides. One side of the blade is smooth and the new cutting edge should be against this side as the rougher, pitted side is unsuitable for forming a good cutting edge.

Be warned: the steel is so hard it can shatter like a piece of glass, with broken fragments flying like shrapnel. Tools made from these blades must be kept for hand use only and never forced, bent, struck with a mallet or used as turning tools.

To remove one rounded end, wrap the blade in a piece of cloth, put it into a vice with the piece to be removed sticking up, and hit it with a hammer sideways on. The blade will snap at the edge of the vice.

You can then grind the blade as required. Always wear eye protection as an added precaution.

You must fit a handle, both for comfort, and to hold the blade securely and prevent it shattering.

You can use nylon reinforced sticky tape, bound round almost up to the cutting edge, and even better is a strip of wood on either side of the blade before binding it with tape.

Rod Naylor

SMALL TOOLS, TOO

In some low-relief designs setting in can be difficult because the wood tends to break out in narrow cross-grain sections.

I avoid the problem by using small firmers and gouges with very thin, almost flexible, walls made from hacksaw blades.

Hand hacksaw blades can be used for 1, 3 and 6mm (⅟₁₆, ⅛ and ¼in) firmers, and power blades can make 6, 10 and 12mm (¼, ⅜ and ½in) tools.

For a handle I use a 100mm (4in) length of 20mm (¾in) dowel. Drill a 25mm (1in) deep hole, of the same diameter as your blade, in one end of the dowel and wedge the blade into the hole with a section of smaller dowel cut in half lengthways.

I find I can cut into walnut (*Juglans spp*) or cherry (*Prunus spp*) up to 3mm (⅛in) without causing splitting, particularly if the section is 6mm (¼in) or more wide.

Used properly, such firmers enable you to set in on the desired line instead of outside it. But, if the wood section remaining is less than 6mm (¼in) wide, particularly across grain, it is advisable to cut in vertically on one side only.

On the other side cut in at a slant to widen the remaining wood. That side can be cut vertical, after grounding out the adjacent wood.

E J Tangerman

N.B. Readers must heed the warnings regarding hacksaw blades given in the previous tip.

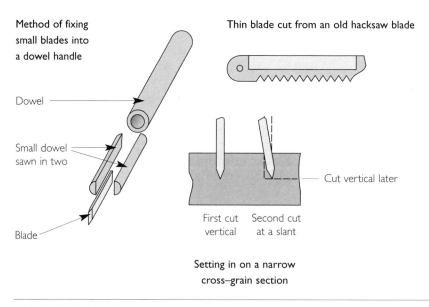

Method of fixing
small blades into
a dowel handle

Thin blade cut from an old hacksaw blade

Dowel

Small dowel
sawn in two

Blade

First cut   Second cut
vertical   at a slant

Cut vertical later

Setting in on a narrow
cross–grain section

SCREW TIGHT

Dowel screws or hanger bolts make good alternatives to carvers' screws, which can be expensive and too bulky for some jobs.

These screws have a wood screw at one end and a machine thread, usually Whitworth, at the other which can be fitted with a washer and wing nut.

They come in a variety of diameters and lengths up to about 75mm (3in).

While they will not pass through a thick bench top they can be put through a hole in a batten or iron bar and clamped in a vice.

C D Atkinson

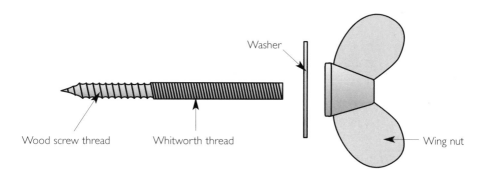

Washer

Wood screw thread   Whitworth thread   Wing nut

TOUGH SCREW

I wanted a large, tough carvers' screw for workholding, but did not want to spend £20 or more buying one. Fortunately I have a friendly local welder who was able to help me.

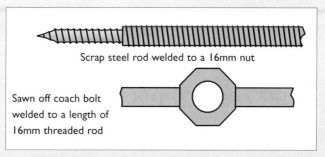

Scrap steel rod welded to a 16mm nut

Sawn off coach bolt welded to a length of 16mm threaded rod

I bought a length of 16mm threaded rod and nuts from my local builders' merchants. This rod is useful for all sorts of clamps and vices. I also bought a large coach screw.

I cut a 200mm (8in) length off the threaded rod, cut about 38mm (1½in) off the end of the coach screw, and filed the cut ends square.

My welder friend welded them together to make my carvers' screw.

I had only the hexagonal nuts for the threaded rod as I could not find any wing nuts with 16mm thread. I thought I would have to use a spanner to tighten them, but my friend welded two bits of scrap steel rod to opposite sides of a nut so I can now turn it by hand.

Ruth Harvey

CARVING SCREW

I made my own carving screw from a length of 10mm (⅜in) threaded rod which you can buy from most hardware and DIY stores, usually complete with a pair of nuts.

I ground a point on one end, but you could use a hacksaw and file.

Drill a 10mm (⅜in) hole in your wood blank to take the rod, and a 5mm (³⁄₁₆in) hole in the far end to take the point. Then, using two nuts locked together, you can screw the rod into the wood with a spanner. I have used this screw on pine (*Pinus spp*), elm (*Ulmus spp*), oak (*Quercus spp*) and mahogany (*Swietenia macrophylla*) with no problems, even on end grain.

Mike Ninham

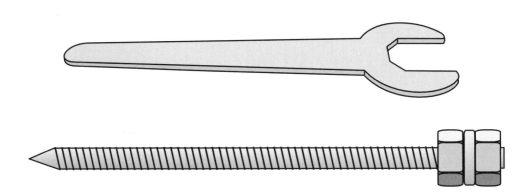

Home made carving screw, which can be inserted with a spanner

HANDY MALLET

A cheap rubber mallet costs only about £2, and I have found the rubber head is ideal to use as a palm mallet in carving. I use the curved and tapered outside edge for light blows and the end for heavier blows.

My rubber mallet had the head fixed on to the handle with a nail, so I cut around the nail head until I had exposed enough to get the pincers in to grip and remove it.

The rubber can be carved with a gouge, so you can cut a groove round the middle to make a thumb grip.

I find the weight just right, but you can lighten the head if you wish, by cutting away more rubber, making the groove bigger.

I also found the hole for the handle was just the right size to fit over the handles of my Henry Taylor chisels. This gives a large area of grip for palm hammering on heavy cuts.

G Hatton

CHOPSTICK TOOLS

As a newcomer to carving, I wanted to make clay maquettes before carving but I did not have any tools to model the clay.

A visit to our local Chinese restaurant provided a pair of plastic chopsticks, which were square at one end and round and tapered the other. I cut one in half with a junior hacksaw and cut the ends to the profiles shown, giving me a total of four modelling tools.

One end of the square section I chamfered diagonally to give a flat blade, and the other end I made like a pointed crochet hook.

With the round section I cut another, smaller, blade on the wide end and another pointed hook on the other end.

Derek Shuttler

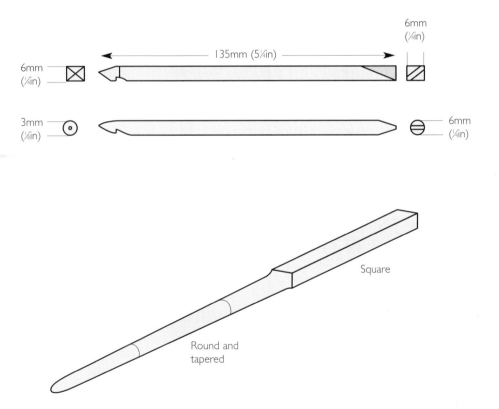

6mm (¼in)

6mm (¼in)

135mm (5¼in)

3mm (⅛in)

6mm (¼in)

Square

Round and tapered

Plastic chopstick, 267mm (10½in) long

SHAPING CUTS

Carvers usually think the radius of a gouge cut is controlled by the radius of the gouge, but this is only partly true.

Grinding back the centre of the gouge will make it form a shallower cut. Also the cut it makes will tend to be more precise and with a smoother finish.

Very shallow gouges tend to have a problem because the corners are prone to digging in and splintering the wood.

If the corners are slightly radiused, then the gouge will be allowed to make a deeper cut without splintering at the edge. A perfectly flat blade with a radiused end will cut a groove like a gouge.

Another way of changing the shape of cut made by a gouge is to change the angle at which it is pushed through the wood.

A wide shallow gouge, when pushed through the wood at an angle of 45°, will make a cut which looks as though it was made by a narrower, U–shaped tool.

Rod Naylor

A A flat blade with a radiused end will cut a groove like a gouge

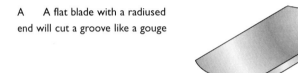

B A wide shallow gouge, held at an angle and pulled through the wood, produces a deep narrow cut like this

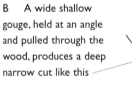 

GRIND INSIDE

Inside ground gouges are often more controllable and require less energy to push than their outside ground equivalents, yet few woodcarvers use inside ground tools.

This is no doubt due to tradition, as inside ground tools used to be tedious to sharpen. But with the widespread use of very hard felt wheels on honing machines they should take only a few seconds to hone to razor sharpness.

I have now reground some of my outside ground tools to convert them to inside ground, as no doubt it will take the manufacturers another century to catch one.

Rod Naylor

MINI POWER STROPS

Smaller power tools, such as the Dremel, can operate at low speeds, which allow them to be used to grind and strop edge tools without too much heat build–up.

You can buy small grinding wheels and felt polishing wheels for them, but you can also make your own leather strops. Take the abrasive sleeve off a sanding drum and glue leather on to the drum to make a power strop.

You can also use a leather disc with a hole poked in the middle and attach a mandrel to make a mini leather strop to get into the smallest palm gouge.

Use stropping compound as if you were hand stropping or using a larger power strop.

Make sure the disk is revolving away from the tool edge, so you do not catch and cut the leather.

Lois Henry

Cut leather to this shape to wrap round the drum

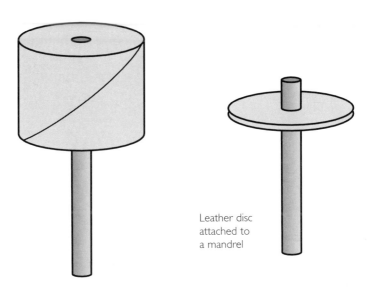

Leather disc attached to a mandrel

Sanding drum strop

STROPPY CASE

My old leather briefcase had a very battered exterior and had reached the end of its working life. However, it was made from good strong leather about 5mm (⅟₁₆in) thick, which I was able to salvage by cutting through the stitching. I used this leather to make some honing strops for my woodcarving tools.

First I made a strop for my flat tools by sticking a piece of leather to a 255 x 100 x 25mm (10 x 4 x 1in) piece of wood.

The leather was cut oversize and stuck to the wood, smooth side down, using contact adhesive. I trimmed the leather when the adhesive had fully set.

The other strops I made were of various diameters for gouges.

To do this, I cut out some pieces of leather about 200-255mm (8-10in) long by 75-100mm (3-4in) wide and bent them round pieces of dowel, broom handle, pencils and knitting needles of various sizes.

My local shoe repairers machine-stitched the leather across a few times, close to the dowel, and this bound the leather and core mandrel tightly together.

The honing aids could then be gripped by the leather tails, thus keeping my fingers well clear of the sharp gouge when honing.

T G Laidler

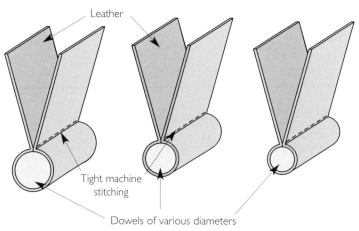

Leather

Tight machine stitching

Dowels of various diameters

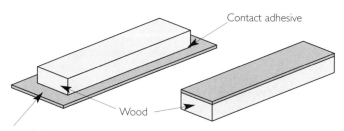

Contact adhesive

Wood

Leather (cut oversize)

MICRO SCORPS

I saw some useful looking blacksmith–made micro scorps in an American woodworking catalogue, but they were rather expensive, so I thought I would make my own.

I had some square steel stock in various sizes and cut 200mm (8in) lengths from four gauges, 6, 8, 10 and 12mm (¼, ⁵⁄₁₆, ⅜ and ½in).

I softened one end of each by heating it to a bright cherry red and leaving it to cool slowly.

I drilled holes close to the end of each rod, each hole 2mm less than the width of the rod. Then I ground down the ends to make them rounded, and chamfered the edges to a cutting profile.

I bent the ends to the required angle and rehardened the steel by heating it to cherry red and quenching it in salt water, stirring vigorously. I then reheated it again to a light straw colour and quenched again.

I fitted wooden handles, and sharpened and honed the ends on a water stone.

Ruth Harvey

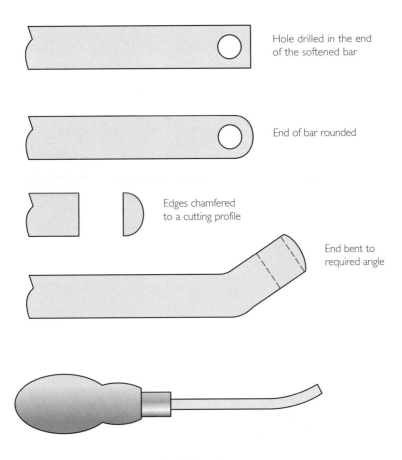

Hole drilled in the end of the softened bar

End of bar rounded

Edges chamfered to a cutting profile

End bent to required angle

Wooden handle fitted

SMALLER SCRAPERS

Scrapers are usually useful tools, but the manufactured range does not seem to cover smaller sizes.

I make a lot of spoons so need mini gooseneck shapes. I make these by grinding down old Stanley knife blades and burnishing them.

A larger version can be made from the Stanley lino cutting blade, which offers a useful range of curves.

The scrapers can either be held in your fingers or used in the Stanley knife handle.

Needle files can also be ground down to make mini versions.

Ruth Harvey

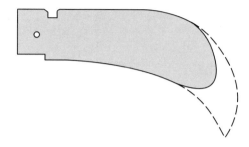

Mini scraper made from a Stanley knife blade

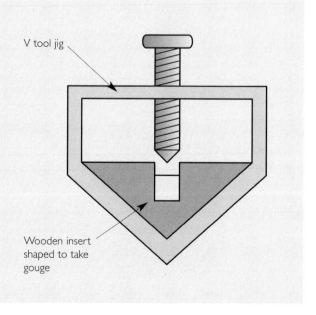

Larger scraper made from a Stanley lino cutting blade

GRINDER TOOL JIG

My old whetstone grinder does not have all the facilities of the new Tormek water cooled grinder but, by using two lengths of strip metal and 100mm (4in) coach bolts, I adapted the tool rest to take the Tormek V tool jig.

Tools other than V tools do not always rest centrally in the jig, so I made some appropriately-shaped wooden inserts – now most tools can be positioned centrally and held before tightening the screw.

John Tybjerg

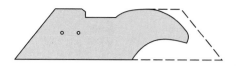

V tool jig

Wooden insert shaped to take gouge

HANDY HANDPIECE

Flexible shaft power tools are very useful but, as with all power tools, you have to be careful they do not harm you or kick, skid or dig in and ruin a delicate piece of work.

I usually reach a point on a carving when I no longer feel comfortable using a power tool, but I still want to use the various steel, diamond and carbide burrs to shape the wood, so I decided to make some handpieces from dowels, to hold the burrs and achieve greater control.

I used 100-125mm (4-5in) long pieces of 12mm (½in) dowel, drilled with holes of a size to take the shanks of the burrs. Used as manual tools these burrs are effective to ream, rasp, riffle, scrape and sand with great control, and allow me to softly stroke away in confined areas.

Later I discovered in a tool store a beech handled holder with a 3-4mm (⅛in) collet. I have also found a pin holder handpiece about 90mm (3½in) x 10mm (⅜in) diameter in a bright nickel finish. This has a 0.5mm cross section slit at each end and various holes which will take any shank size, from a fine needle through to over 3mm (⅛in). It will also take a coping saw and small hacksaw blade.

Of course, you can buy burrs to use in a handpiece, even if you do not have a flexible power drive.

Mike Cuomo

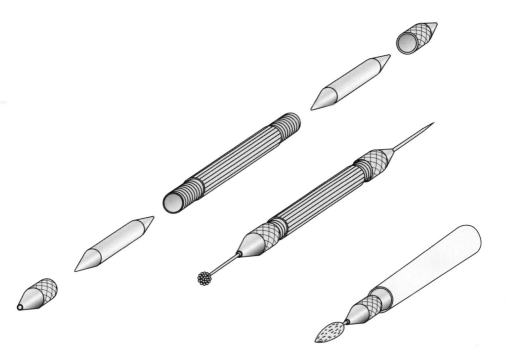

The pin holder, exploded view (top) and assembled (middle), with the beech handled holder (bottom)

Techniques

STRAIGHTEN STICKS

If you carve walking sticks, they often need to be straightened. This is not easy without a steamer, but I have found using an electric hot air paint stripper works extremely well.

Direct the jet of hot air at the area to be straightened, slowly moving it up and down and round the stick so the whole area gets very hot. Then bend the stick in the opposite direction to the bend you want to lose, repeating the heating process as necessary.

There is no fuss, no mess, and the stick does not get burnt so long as the hot air is not applied to a single area for too long.

Paul Goodrick

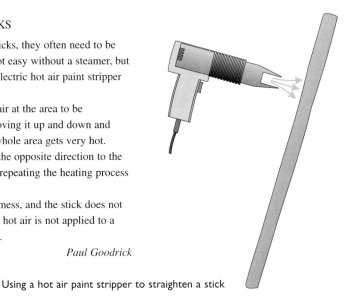

Using a hot air paint stripper to straighten a stick

STOP BLISTERS

If you get blisters or sore patches on your hands and fingers when carving, wrap plastic insulating tape round the vulnerable parts.

When you finish carving, unwind the tape and keep it, as it can be used over and over again without wearing out.

I have found I can wash my hands without the tape getting soggy, and it does not leave a sticky mess on my hands when I take it off.

Pamela Stewart-Pearson

CHEAP OIL

I use vegetable oil to preserve wood. It soaks well in, cares for it, and creates a natural look.

Large quantities can be bought quite cheaply, saving money on proprietary brands of wood preservative. My husband even uses it on the garden shed and fence and, being vegetable, it does not harm plants.

We save our cooking oil after we have finished with it in the kitchen, strain it and use it as a second application on the fence.

Valerie Thome

NATIVITY SCENE

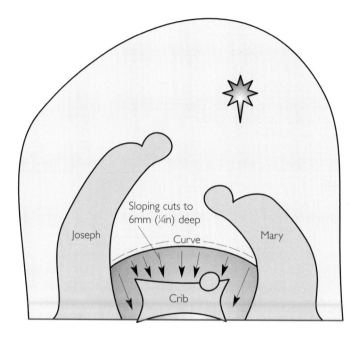

Faced with a load of flat beech (Fagus sylvatica) offcuts from relief carvings, I decided to make some Nativity scenes suitable for Christmas gifts. I wanted something simple but effective, and hopefully enduring.

I drew a simple Nativity scene and made photocopies of different sizes to suit the pieces of wood I had available.

I transferred the photocopied drawings on to the wood offcuts using carbon paper, and sawed round the outlines of the shapes.

I next incised the outlines of Mary, Joseph, the crib and the star with a V tool, deliberately leaving the stylised figures faceless for effect.

To create an impression of depth, I incised a curve above the crib and gouged out from the edge of the curve and the lower outlines of Mary and Joseph, sloping inwards to the crib, to a depth of about 6mm (¼in).

I lightly sanded the outer edge and front surface, and with the thinner offcuts I glued a short supporting length of wood along the base at the back so they could be freestanding.

I finished the plaques with Danish oil, and they made excellent gifts.

Patricia Vardigans

BURR EDGE

Here is an idea for getting into those awkward recesses on a carving where the grain always seems to run the wrong way.

Select an ordinary carpenters' chisel of the most convenient width, and turn its edge with a ticketer, in the same way as you would burr the edge of a cabinet scraper. Use this to scrape out the wood, rather than cutting into the grain. You will find it removes the material very easily.

To restore a sharp edge to the tool simply wipe it on an oil stone, and no damage is done.

Ted Jeffery

CUTTING OUT BIG BLOCKS

It is difficult to cut out a large block to shape for a carving if it is too big to fit in a bandsaw.

I cut a flat surface on the block and draw the design on it. Next, I use an electric drill, preferably in a stand, and drill a series of holes round the outline to cut out the shape.

I then simply cut the back of the block flat and place the block on the stand for drilling. Once a hole has been accurately started you can deepen it by holding the drill freehand.

Rod Naylor

ON THE MAT

When finishing the fine detail of a carving it is much easier if you remove your work from its clamp and work on it in good daylight near a window.

To hold your carving, buy a metre or two of rubber backing material from a carpet shop, the type used to stop rugs slipping.

When this is folded and placed over a cushion, it makes a really firm support on which to manoeuvre your carving.

Pamela Stewart-Pearson

MOULDING MITRES

When carving lengths of moulding, deciding the exact position of a mitre in the design can be tedious. You can try making drawings, but this requires a lot to see how each section will look.

A much quicker and easier way is to simply place a mirror on its edge on the moulding, at an angle of 45°. Slide the mirror along the pattern to instantly see how the design will change as it goes round the bend.

Rod Naylor

Arrow in a Bottle

For decades I have used the Japanese technique of 'ukibori', using a suitably shaped tool to produce the warts on toads or scales on snakes. A similar technique, at least 100 years old, is used for putting an arrow through a small hole in a target or into a long-necked bottle.

The arrow is made of soft wood, which is thoroughly soaked in warm water, then compressed in a vice until the head is small enough to go through the opening. When the wood dries, the arrow head swells back to its original size and shape to mystify beholders.

Japanese panel carvers sometimes carve under water. This makes carving easier, reduces the likelihood of splitting, and floats chips away as they are cut.

Carving a fan is also done by soaking the soft wood blank before splitting and interlocking the leaves.

E J Tangerman

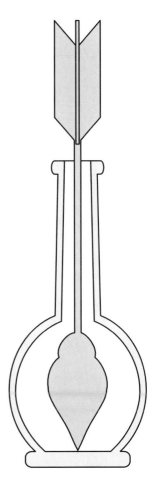

Arrow in a bottle – all done with water

Hide glue lines

Carvers often make large carvings by laminating smaller blocks of wood together, but these pieces are sometimes ruined by glue lines, which become visible after polishing.

A perfect joint can be made by adding a small amount of powder pigment to the adhesive. For example, a little white and a trace of yellow ochre in the glue can be used for satinwood (*Chloroxylon swietenia*).

Experiment with scrap wood first, and remember to match the glue to the colour the wood will become after it is polished.

Rod Naylor

STRONG JOINT

Sometimes you need to join large pieces of wood together for a carving, and it may not be possible to cramp up, or you may need extra strength in the joint.

Handrail bolts for bolting wood together are now almost impossible to obtain, so I use threaded rod, from 6–12mm (¼–½in), with T nuts and wing nuts for strengthening the glue joint.

Make sure the edges of the wood to be joined fit together smoothly, then drill 25mm (1in) diameter holes in the back of each piece to a depth of just over half the thickness.

Drill a hole to fit the shank of the T nut in one piece, and a hole for the threaded rod in the other.

Cut off a 75mm (3in) length of threaded rod, and grind a point on one end to give a good start to the nut. Position the T nut down one hole with tweezers or long-nosed pliers and pull it into place with the rod and wing nut. (If you do not have a T nut you can use ordinary square or hexagonal nuts, but they will have to be wedged to stop them turning.)

If it all fits together well, remove the wing nut and glue the wood together. Then put a washer and wing nut back on the end of the rod and tap the nut round with a punch until it is fully tightened.

Cut a diamond plug – or turn a round plug – to fill the holes, and glue into position.

An alternative is to use a hanger bolt, which has a wood screw on one end and a metal thread on the other. In this case you screw the wood screw into one piece of wood and need drill only one 25mm (1in) hole for the wing nut.

John Warner

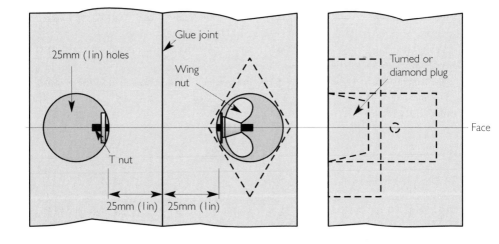

View from the back   View from the side

Stick 'em up

When working on small items like carved boxes it is best to separate the lid from the base and dig out the inside waste before carving the outside decoration.

You then need to hold the two halves together while you carve the outside.

You can do this with hot melt glue or PVA glue and paper, but these methods leave glue in the wood which can hinder finishing.

I prefer to stick the halves together with wax, either from a white candle or from the thick layer used to seal the ends of wood blanks.

To enable the wax to penetrate the wood a little you must pre-warm the wood. Put it in a warm (not hot) oven for a few minutes, or in a microwave for a few seconds until the wood is warm but not too hot to hold.

Drip the molten wax on to one surface and press the other half on to it. Secure the halves together lightly with rubber bands, until the wax cools and sets.

When the carving is completed, heat the wood as before to melt the wax, separate the halves and wipe off the wax.

You can clean off the wax with a solvent such as paraffin, petrol or methylated spirits, but I find the wax leaves no trace if I finish the carving with wax or oil.

Russell Parry

Larger image

As a novice woodcarver, my first project was to carve a Welsh springer spaniel, helped by a small photograph.

I wanted to enlarge the image three or four times, so I traced round the spaniel's outline on the photograph, and made a cardboard template.

I put the template on a photographic enlarger and projected the enlarged image on to the carving block, then marked out the shape on the block. I could have used the photograph negative of course.

Alternatively, you could use a photocopier to enlarge the image.

W E Protheroe

Get a grip

I often hold a carving chisel between my thumb and forefinger, near the cutting edge, and use it like a pen for fine cutting. This is a technique shown me by Zoë Gertner.

Because I have dry hands, I found it difficult to grip the steel shaft until I discovered cheap and simple rubber thimbles called Thimblettes. These are sold in various sizes by stationers' shops, and are used for turning pages, counting banknotes, etc.

Peter Valentine

DRYING STICKS

Among my carving interests is simple stickmaking, and I needed to devise a way of leaving the sticks to dry after oiling and waxing without them touching each other or anything else.

I hammered several long, thin nails into the edge of a high shelf in the workshop. Now, before oiling and waxing, I tap a 15mm (⅝in) panel pin into the bottom of each stick. I tie a knot round the pin with a short length of string, loop the other end of the string over a nail in the shelf, and the stick can hang to dry.

I can now hang several sticks up to dry at once.

Patricia Vardigans

HOUSE NAMES

Carvers are often asked to produce house names and numbers, even though they may have insufficient knowledge of lettering.

However, problems are most likely to arise with the painting of the letters. Paint seems to creep along the grain of the wood under the surface and can re-appear later as coloured specks under the finish.

A way of preventing this is to varnish the letters and surrounding surface before painting. This not only prevents the paint penetrating the grain but also allows you to be freer with the paint, as any overlapping the edge of the letters can be wiped off easily.

Once everything is thoroughly dry, you sand the whole surface flat producing beautifully sharp-edged letters which can be treated with your chosen finish.

I have used this method for some time without problems, particularly when finishing with oil or a microporous finish.

Peter Benson

SHARP SCRAPERS

My worst nightmare used to be trying to sharpen small scrapers for smoothing hardwood carvings.

Despite the laws laid down by generations of textbooks, I now use a honing machine with paper or very hard felt wheels.

I admit the result is not so good as a perfectly sharpened scraper, but I never learned how to get the ultimate edge on a scraper in less than five seconds.

Rod Naylor

JOINT IDEA

Many carvers joint parts together, such as fixing flower heads to stalks, but ordinary dowels are often too thick to use.

Instead you can use cocktail sticks, kebab sticks, or chopsticks which are available from kitchen shops or supermarkets. Bamboo is the best material.

Rod Naylor

BRING DRAWINGS TO LIFE

When working up commission proposals for presentation to clients I include a full-scale drawing but, because many people find it hard to visualise a three-dimensional carving from a flat piece of paper, I often shade my drawings in an attempt to help them.

I have discovered that, by using a black or dark brown coloured pencil, the drawing does not smudge the way graphite or charcoal pencils do.

The coloured pencil has a wax-based binder so it sticks to the paper, and the rendering photocopies and faxes well, too.

Fred Wilbur

OIL SAVER

If you leave oil, such as tung oil, in a jar or bottle it will form a skin over the top.

To prevent this, store the oil in a soft plastic bottle such as a clean washing up liquid bottle, and squeeze out all the air before replacing the cap.

As well as preserving the oil, this gives you a handy container, which will dispense oil in a controlled way.

E Chick

NO MORE CARBON

Many carvers transfer a drawing to a piece of wood with carbon paper before sawing out the outline and starting to carve. The problem is that within minutes you have carved away all the drawing of the positions of features such as eyes, mouth and so on.

I have overcome this problem by mounting an inexpensive opaque projector on an overhead beam. This projects my drawing down on to the workbench. If you position your work on the bench and draw a pencil line round it, you can return any time later and place your work on the pencilled outline. Then just turn on the projector and the drawing will be shown on the work.

My callipers are now gathering dust.

Kenneth Dubin

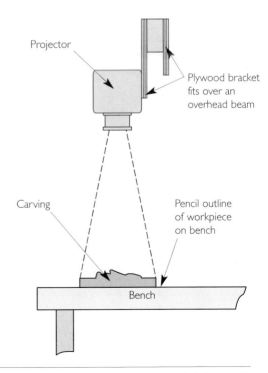

Projector

Plywood bracket
fits over an
overhead beam

Carving

Pencil outline
of workpiece
on bench

Bench

Clamps and workholders

TILTING CLAMP

To hold wood for relief carvings I use a holding board with some toggle clamps.

At first I held the board in my bench vice, but later I made up a tilt and swivel mount from some offcuts, and screwed the holding board to the tilting block.

The whole unit can be held in a vice or clamped to the bench. For carving in the round I use a double ended screw or hangar bolt fitted into the tilting block. This makes a cheap and sturdy carvers' clamp.

A J Dale

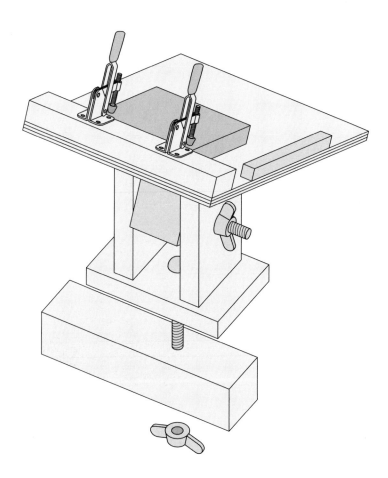

Holding board

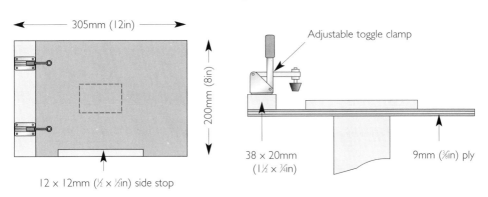

305mm (12in)

200mm (8in)

Adjustable toggle clamp

38 × 20mm
(1½ × ¾in)

9mm (⅜in) ply

12 × 12mm (½ × ½in) side stop

Tilt and swivel mount

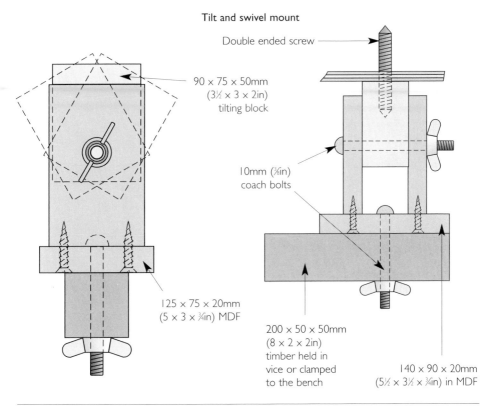

Double ended screw

90 × 75 × 50mm
(3½ × 3 × 2in)
tilting block

10mm (⅜in)
coach bolts

125 × 75 × 20mm
(5 × 3 × ¾in) MDF

200 × 50 × 50mm
(8 × 2 × 2in)
timber held in
vice or clamped
to the bench

140 × 90 × 20mm
(5½ × 3½ × ¾in) in MDF

Holding Aid

If you need to carve a thin, delicate piece of wood such as a violin profile, it can be difficult to hold the piece securely without damaging it.

I made a mould to hold the piece using a simple wooden tray. The profile was 20mm (¾in) thick so I used a tray 25mm (1in) deep.

I made some builders' finishing plaster and filled the tray three quarters full, then covered it with a sheet of cling film.

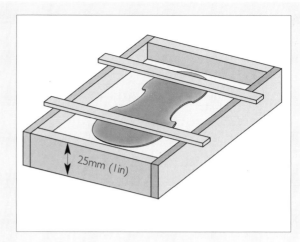

Next I pressed the wood down into the plaster, tapping it lightly to ensure it bedded in well all over.

Once the profile was level with the top, I fixed two battens over the tray to hold the profile securely.

I removed the profile after about an hour and left the plaster to fully set overnight.

The next day I had a perfect mould to hold and support the profile securely while carving it. One of the battens can be used to secure the wood in place.

George Hibbs

Clamp Pads

Carvers use lots of clamps for holding wood while carving or gluing pieces together, but you have to be careful or the clamps can leave unsightly marks on the wood.

To prevent this you can put bits of cardboard, hardboard or thin ply between the clamp and the wood, but this is fiddly and the bits tend to fall out as you tighten the clamp.

Now I collect all the plastic tops from bottles and other containers and keep them in a jar. When clamping I find one of the right size to fit over the shoe of the clamp.

For smaller clamps you can use the tops of plastic film containers.

George Coxwell

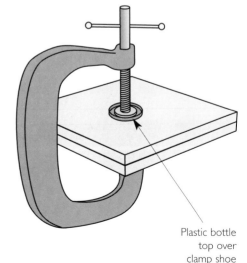

Plastic bottle top over clamp shoe

Budget Carving Horse

As I am unable to stand to carve for long and, having limited cash resources, I decided to make a heavy duty carving horse from scrap, so I could sit and carve in comfort.

Previously I used an old saw horse, but it was not really big or sturdy enough for the job.

The top is a 815mm (32in) long piece of 230 x 75mm (9 x 3in) old floor joist, rescued from the tip.

The bigger and heavier the wood, the more stable and solid the carving horse will be, but you could use anything down to about 150 x 50mm (6 x 2in) and it would still be strong enough.

I measured in 150mm (6in) from each end and cut housing joints for the four legs. This was the only difficult bit, as the joints are compound angles.

These are not critical, provided the horse is stable and does not fall over, but I found 75° to the side and 60° forwards and back was about right.

The housings needed to be deep enough to take the legs, which were made from 75 x 38mm (3 x 1½in) pieces of scrap wood.

My legs are 600mm (23½in) long, but you can cut yours to a length to suit yourself.

The legs were screwed and glued in and, for extra strength and stability, I fixed leg braces. These were 50 x 20mm (2 x ¾in) lengths of scrap wood, screwed on 75mm (3in) up from the bottom of the legs. To one end of the horse I coach-bolted a 75mm (3in) thick piece of 150 x 125mm (6 x 5in) wood to give more height, and then fixed my multi-angle to that with coach screws.

I also drilled a hole in the block for a carving screw.

A carpet offcut and a soft cushion was all that was then needed to provide a cheap and comfortable carving horse.

Mine has had a lot of use and has stood up to much heavy work.

Mike Ninham

Carving horse made from scrap wood

CAM CLAMP

When carving a small, irregular-shaped fragile piece I wanted a simple, quick-release way of holding the work on a chipboard backing board so I could move the item round while carving.

I could have used double-sided sticky tape, but this would not have allowed much manoeuvrability of the workpiece, and there would also have been the danger of breaking the carving when prizing it off the backing board.

I made up this cam clamp to hold the work. The workpiece is located with four short pieces of 12mm (½in) diameter dowel, each shorter than the depth of the workpiece.

The dowel pieces are screwed to the backing board, with the chipboard screws countersunk below the top surface of the dowels.

The dowel rods can of course be moved to accommodate any shape of carving, and can be placed inside a pierced carving.

The cam lever is secured with a chipboard screw and washer, tightened just pinch-tight.

The shape of the cam lever means a workpiece can be quickly and easily secured and released.

W R Markham

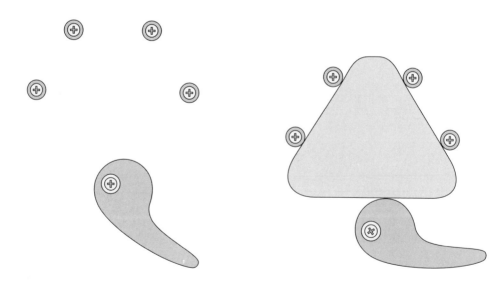

STEEL HOLDER

I have designed and made this carving clamp from tubular steel. It also requires some flanged steel blocks with brass collets, but the cost is not high and, once assembled, it makes the most solid clamping fixture I have ever tried.

Any number of blocks and collets may be used, and the steel tube can be any length, so the clamp will take any size piece.

It is extremely rigid when bolted to the bench, and the workpiece is held absolutely solid. The brass collets are locked with Allen screws.

Work is most secure when held vertically by two or more blocks, but it can also be held horizontally.

George Mateer

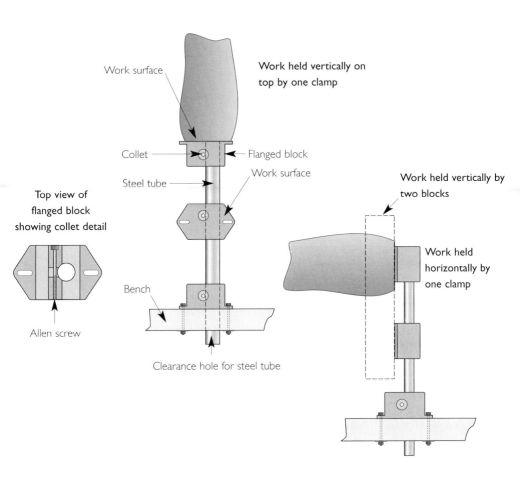

Work surface

Work held vertically on
top by one clamp

Collet

Flanged block

Steel tube

Work surface

Work held vertically by
two blocks

Top view of
flanged block
showing collet detail

Work held
horizontally by
one clamp

Allen screw

Bench

Clearance hole for steel tube

CLEAT TABLE

I am sure many people carve on tables which must not be damaged, as I have had to when teaching classes over the years.

This means you cannot nail or screw cleats to the table top to hold your workpiece panel in place, and a clamp tends to get in the way.

As a result I have used a plate, which is simply a bench stop or hook, with notched cleats on the top and one side.

The plate can be made from a piece of plywood a bit larger than the panels you want to carve. Fix a batten across the underneath of the near end to catch against the table edge.

If you are carving small panels, you can clamp the plate to the table without the clamp being too close to the work.

You can also use plastic netting or webbing from carpet shops, designed to stop small rugs from slipping. This works well on panels of about 306 x 230mm (12 x 9in) or larger.

Smaller panels can be tacked to a larger board to hold them on the webbing.

E J Tangerman

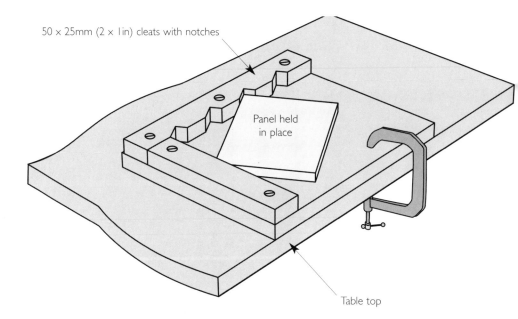

50 x 25mm (2 x 1in) cleats with notches

Panel held in place

Table top

Bench plate or hook 380 x 305 x 25mm (15 x 12 x 1in)

BENCH AID

I made myself a woodworking and carving bench, and a jig and clamp for use on it.

The jig is a shooting board, with a range of holes in it to take plastic shelf brackets available from DIY stores. The holes are opened out underneath so they can also take bolts.

The clamp is made from two wooden wedges bolted together.

The jig and clamp are held to the bench with a metal holdfast. Plastic furniture wedges or level blocks are useful for packing.

This enables me to adjust small carvings to a wide variety of positions for carving.

A V Wells

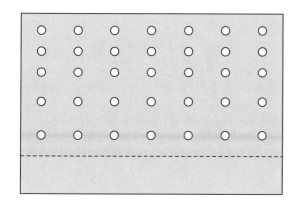

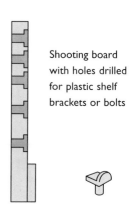

Shooting board with holes drilled for plastic shelf brackets or bolts

Shelf bracket

Wedges

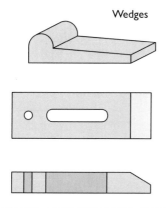

Furniture wedge or level block

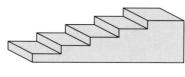

VICE SUPPORT

When holding odd-shaped carvings in a wood vice it is easy to over-tighten the vice to hold the carving securely. This may bruise the wood or even damage the piece.

To improve the clamping of uneven forms I cut some 50 x 25 x 6mm (2 x 1 x ¼in) hardwood strips (variable sizes) and cut a full radius on the end of each.

I lay the strips on their sides, held loosely in a C clamp, and adjust them so they fit the shape of the carving. Then I tighten the clamp securely.

When I place the clamped strips in the vice they support the carving, so I can reduce the side pressure needed to hold it firmly for carving.

Chris Brown

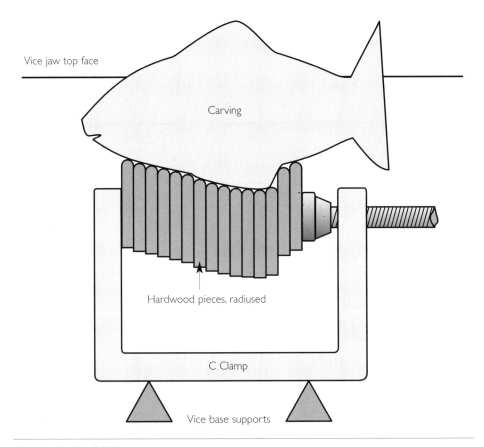

Vice jaw top face

Carving

Hardwood pieces, radiused

C Clamp

Vice base supports

CLAMP FOR ODD SHAPES

Holding odd shaped pieces for carving is always a challenge. A bench vice is awkward and often holds the workpiece at the wrong angle.

This is an idea for an easy-to-make clamp to remedy the situation. The two main advantages of this are the work is held at a comfortable angle for working and, although it is held securely, it is easy to rotate as needed.

To use the clamp I push the workpiece up against the nail on the fixed end, slide the moveable end up snugly and tighten the wing nut.

Finally I give two turns of the screw on the movable end, to secure the workpiece, and I am ready to carve.

You will obviously need to allow some spare wood at each end of the workpiece to allow for the holes left by the nail and screw.

R B Hines

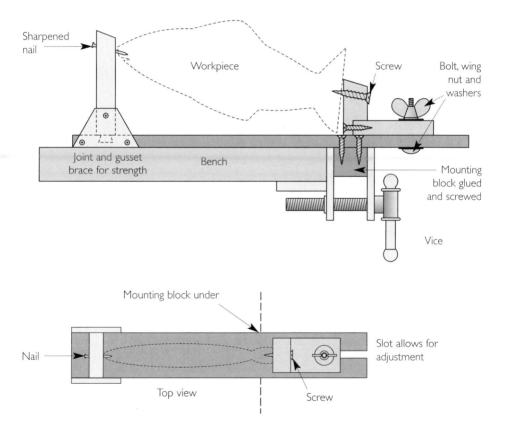

Carving clamp for odd shapes

HANDY CLAMP

I have to carve from a seated position, so I wanted a clamp I could adjust easily without having to get up and move around the bench.

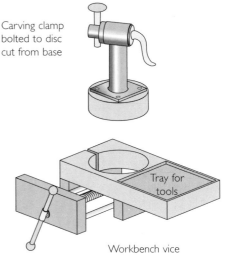

Carving clamp bolted to disc cut from base

I came up with this solution, which holds a standard carving clamp in a workbench vice.

The base is a 300 x 150 x 38mm (12 x 6 x 1½in) piece of ash (*Fraxinus spp*). If you use a longer piece, it can also provide a tray for your carving tools.

Near one end I cut out a 125mm (5in) disc as shown and bolted my carving clamp to that. A small gap was then sawn from the circular hole to the outside of the base.

This allows the clamp to be easily rotated, and simply tightening the bench vice locks it.

Tray for tools

Workbench vice

The base is held in the vice with a simple bracket screwed on underneath. The whole thing can be quickly removed by unhooking the bracket from the vice.

Edwin Reetham

CARVING SEAT

I have seen a number of combination carving stools and vices on the market, and thought I could adapt my Superjaws to make a similar device.

I usually stand when using the Superjaws, but thought sitting on it could be more comfortable for smaller carvings.

To make the seat I welded a piece of rolled H-section steel to an old exercise bike saddle. The steel section slips into the rear of the sliding rear jaw of the Superjaws.

I am around 1.8m (6ft) tall, and my feet reach the ground, so I can 'stand seated' at the jaws, but shorter people may need to rest their feet on a block.

Of course you cannot use the seat when the rear jaw is extended beyond a safe limit for balance.

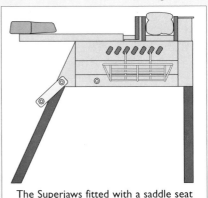

The Superjaws fitted with a saddle seat

The Superjaws comes with a handy tool tray where you can keep your carving chisels.

Glenn Roberts

CORK CLAMP

The jaws of a vice, or metal and plastic clamps can easily mark wood, but a simple and effective way of holding wood securely in a vice or clamp without marking is to use wine bottle corks as a buffer.

As cork is much softer than wood it does not cause damage and will also mould itself to the shape of the carving.

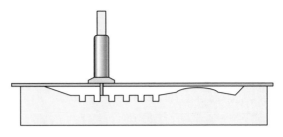

Using corks to hold a carving in a vice

Even with the vice tightened considerably it is the cork which squashes rather than the wood, and it is surprising how tight a grip can be obtained.

It is best to use corks from sparkling wine as they have a wider cross section.

Slit the cork down the middle with a sharp knife and wedge your carving in the holding device between the two halves of the cork. With regular use the corks flatten out, and you can use several corks if necessary for a large carving.

You can usually hold the cork in position while you tighten the vice or clamp, but you can stick the cork to the wood with a dab of glue.

Afterwards pull the cork off and remove any remaining pieces with a chisel.

An extra advantage of using cork with a clamp is that contacting metal or plastic does not damage your tools.

Paul Goodrick

HOLD IT

Here is a fast, flexible and adaptable method for holding wood for carving on the bench. It is particularly suitable for use with relief carvings.

First make a right-angled tri-square from wood about 20mm (¾in) thick. This can then be held on the workbench with a bench holdfast, clamp or even screwed down.

The tri-square then holds the wood so you can push against it while carving, and the workpiece can be quickly and easily turned to suit the grain or angle of cut.

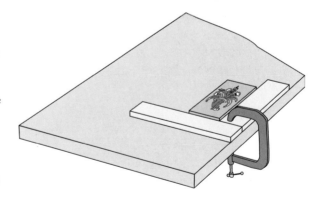

Tri-square and holdfast help relief carving

Making a jig/frame with three sides instead of two, and two right-angled joints can extend this idea. The workpiece can then by pushed into the most convenient angle without having to move the frame.

Hugh Thomas

VICE WORKHOLDER

I have a large, solid, engineering vice with swivel action. It is strong and useful, but I wanted to make it more versatile for holding carvings.

I got two 150 x 150mm (6 x 6in) plates of 6mm (¼in) mild steel, drilled with evenly-spaced 6mm (¼in) holes, like a pegboard.

I got my friendly local welder to weld the plates to the tops of the vice jaws. Used with small pegs, which I have cut to fit the holes, and some wooden packing pieces and wedges, I now have a versatile clamp which will hold quite large irregular panels and other awkward shapes.

Ruth Harvey

Pegs

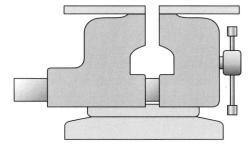

Plates fixed to engineering vice

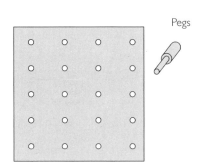

Steel plates 150 x 150mm
(6 x 6in) drilled with 6mm (¼in) holes

CLAMP IDEA

I made a clamp for woodcarving using an old wig clamp, available from wig makers or suppliers for £6-£7, and a hanger bolt.

The top portion of the wig clamp was cut off, and a hole drilled and tapped to take the bolt.

The hanger bolt has a machine screw on one end, which I screwed into the clamp, and a wood screw on the other end, which screwed into the carving block.

The clamp can be attached to a bench or table, and the joint allows it to be adjusted.

Joannes Teernstra

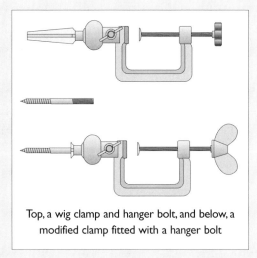

Top, a wig clamp and hanger bolt, and below, a modified clamp fitted with a hanger bolt

KINDER CHOPS

The Tiranti Scopas Chops carvers' vice has been around for a long time, I believe for most of this century, and so there must be thousands of these vices in use around the world.

It is ideal when wood has to be held without danger of being crushed or marked, as the jaws are cushioned. But it has one distinct drawback. The threaded rod that screws the jaws together or apart is so located that the thread can easily come into contact with the carving, causing deep score marks on the wood surface.

This invariably happens when you approach the finishing stage of a carving, when the wood is smooth. It can be a real nuisance, as the damage can be difficult to eradicate without a lot of scraping and sanding.

Over the years I have tried various solutions, such as wrapping the rod in cloth or using pieces of cardboard tubes such as toilet roll or kitchen roll centres. But whatever I have used invariably falls off just at the critical moment.

Now I have found the answer, in the form of foam insulation tubing used to insulate water pipes. This is 55mm (2¼in) diameter externally and 30mm (1⅛in) internally and available from most DIY stores.

The length you need depends on how big the carving is, and how wide open the jaws of the chops need to be.

It is easy to cut, fitting is no problem, and it stays in place without trouble.

Jeremy Williams

Using pipe insulation to protect carvings from a vice screw thread

MIRROR CLAMP

As a pensioner I am always looking for woodcarving aids I can make cheaply.

In a scrap yard I found an old car side mirror holder with a ball joint enabling it to be turned to almost any angle. I bought this for 50p and screwed it to a block of wood, which I can hold in a vice. This makes a great holder for small carvings.

R A Bromley

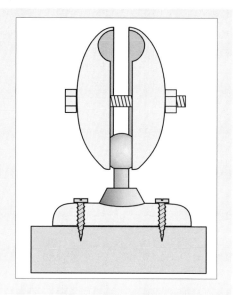

The ball joint mirror holder made into a carving clamp

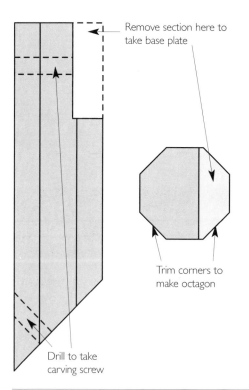

Remove section here to take base plate

Trim corners to make octagon

Drill to take carving screw

CARVING POST

This idea for a carving post is a development of the idea of using a piece of scrap wood held in a vice for holding a carving.

I used a 305mm (12in) long piece of 80mm (3⅛in) square hardwood, trimmed on the corners to make an octagon cross section.

I cut one end off at 45°, and removed a section about 15mm (⅝in) deep and 80mm (3⅛in) down the length from the other end.

This enabled a base plate to be bolted or screwed on to the top of the wood, the side, or at 45°.

These combinations, together with the eight sides of the post, allow access to a carving from almost any angle.

You can also drill a hole through the post to take a carving screw.

John Tybjerg

Handy workholder

Using a normal workbench for carving can give you backache, so carvers sometimes put their work on a post, held in a vice, to raise it higher.

My idea is for a workholder to secure the work to the top of the post.

A slotted block is screwed to the underside of the carving block. The rebated slot takes a bolt, which is tightened to the post. The bolt is tightened with a ring or socket spanner through an access slot in the post (see illustration).

You can then adjust the post in the vice to the height and angle required, and turn the top block and workpiece through 360°.

B J Walker

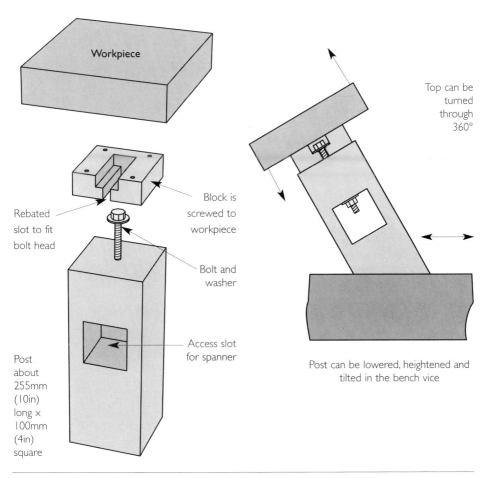

Workpiece

Block is screwed to workpiece

Rebated slot to fit bolt head

Bolt and washer

Access slot for spanner

Post about 255mm (10in) long × 100mm (4in) square

Top can be turned through 360°

Post can be lowered, heightened and tilted in the bench vice

BEAN BAG HOLDER

Sometimes it is difficult to hold a carving securely for the finishing cuts.

When finish sanding a fish I realized with horror I had forgotten to cut in the gills before cutting it free from its support.

It was a problem holding the fish flat and still while cutting the gills with a small V tool or chip carving knife, as the fish was oval and had delicate fins and tail.

Using a bag of rice to hold a fish carving

I did not want to risk holding the carving for fear of damage to my hands or the fish.

I realized I needed a miniature bean bag, and found a half full plastic bag of rice. This enabled the fish to be carefully but firmly bedded down and the job was soon finished.

Although the plastic bag did not slip, a small soft leather or canvas bag filled with lentils, rice or sand would be better.

John Beart

CRADLE HOLDER

Round objects are difficult to hold and clamp, so can be a chore to carve. And, if you do manage to clamp them, it is really inconvenient to re-adjust them each time you need to move them a bit while carving.

To cope with this I have devised this carving cradle, which is simply a V-shaped box made from scrap boards. It's a bit like a book rack, and sits on my bench.

Each trough-like cradle is made to a size to suit the carving and, as the boards are screwed, they can easily be taken apart and adjusted for the next carving.

R B Himes

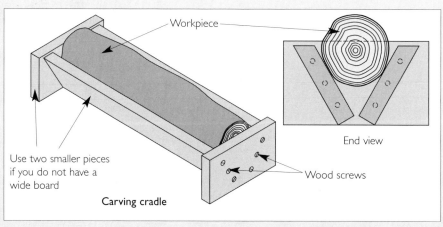

Workpiece

End view

Use two smaller pieces if you do not have a wide board

Wood screws

Carving cradle

CARVING BENCH

As a low-income pensioner, I cannot afford commercially-produced carving benches and workholders for relief carving, so I made my own by adapting a sturdy home-made long wooden stool with four splayed legs.

On one end I mounted an adjustable clamp I had bought cheaply. This is like a sash cramp when clamped onto the edge of a bench.

I screwed a 280 x 190 x 50mm (11 x 7½ x 2in) piece of wood with rounded corners to the circular clamp plate. This provided a solid blackboard for my small to medium-sized relief carvings.

The carvings are secured to the backboard with five pieces of double-sided adhesive tape, one in each corner and one in the middle.

This bench is light and can easily be dismantled for transporting, and the clamp can be removed and fixed to a table if I want to carve standing.

Patricia Vardigans

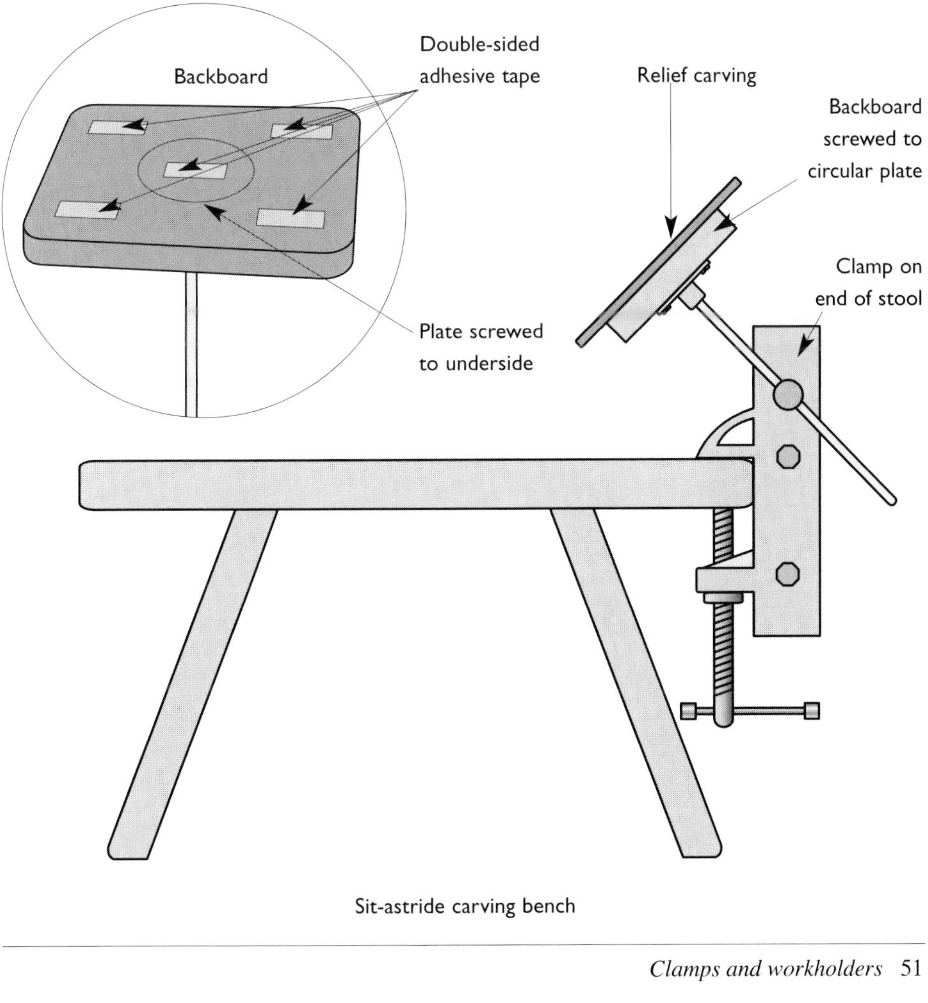

Backboard

Double-sided adhesive tape

Relief carving

Backboard screwed to circular plate

Clamp on end of stool

Plate screwed to underside

Sit-astride carving bench

Sanding and abrasives

SANDING BELT

I have a Black & Decker
Powerfile, which is very useful for
rough sanding but has limited use
on curved surfaces.

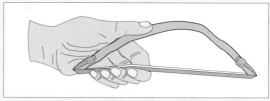

You can use the Powerfile
sanding belts for sanding curved surfaces if you cut the loop and hold one end in each hand,
pulling the belt back and forwards over the wood. The trouble with this is it is difficult to control
the direction and pressure of sanding.

My solution is to attach the belt to a thin, springy green wood branch and hold it as in the
drawing.

You can adjust the tension and pressure of sanding by squeezing the belt and bow with your hand.

As you can get into tight, awkward corners with the tip of the bow, it makes the chore of
sanding curved surfaces a lot easier, without wearing out your finger tips.

Geoff Morgan

EXTRACTION

It is important to use a dust extraction system when using power tools, such as carbide burrs or
sanding drums which produce fine dust, but commercial systems are expensive.

I made a large funnel by cutting up an old 5 litre plastic bottle, and attached a vacuum cleaner hose
to the top.

If the top is too small, you can seal the gap with some sticky tape.

N.B. You should also wear a mask or respirator.

Rod Naylor

SMOOTHING STRIP

Engineers use strips of aluminium oxide abrasive cloth for polishing shafts and other round
components. It comes in various grades, in rolls 25mm (1in) wide and several yards long, and
can be cut into thinner strips.

I use lengths about 610mm (24in) long, which are ideal for sanding walking sticks held in a
vice, or for reaching other inaccessible places on carvings.

You should not use long lengths with a lathe or power tools, as they could get caught up.

G Mateer

ABRASIVE PADS

There are lots of commercially made abrasive devices on the market, but here is my home-made version.

You can buy nylon pad pan scourers, which are impregnated with abrasives of various grades. If you trap a disc of this material between two large washers on a spindle, such as a threaded rod or bolt, you can use this in an electric drill.

A single disc forms a narrow wheel, suitable for smoothing the bottoms of grooves. Several discs or rectangular strips, placed side by side, are more suitable for general work.

Rod Naylor

USE FOR LOLLY STICKS

Lolly sticks, with pieces of various grades of abrasive paper stuck to them, make good tools for sanding in tight places.

Remember to write the grit grade of abrasive on the end of the stick.

R A Bromley

COLOUR MATCH

When finishing a carving, it is a good idea to use an abrasive material the same colour as your workpiece.

For mahogany, I use a piece of old brick which is softer and less gritty than a new one.

Ebony and black buffalo horn can be given a lustre with charcoal, and ivory-type materials take an excellent polish from whiting.

Dust from the abrasive acts as a filler and hides small blemishes rather than highlighting them.

Rod Naylor

SANDING AID

Some sanding systems consist of a textured metal plate fixed to a plastic handle. These are difficult to fit into tight spaces or round corners, as they are not very flexible.

What I have done is to stick the abrasive plate on to a thin aluminium plate. This can be bent to shape to fit into tight corners or curved surfaces, and can also be cut into thin strips.

J M Blaik

BENCH SANDER

My interest in decoy duck carving started with a
visit to America and, as I struggled with various
hand sanding devices and drill attachments, I
yearned for the powerful drum sanders I had seen
in American workshops. These home-made
devices consisted of a small motor attached to the
bench with a 230mm (9in) or 280mm (11in)
pneumatic drum fixed to the spindle. They
speeded the process we all find so tedious.

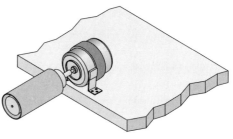

The bench sander fixed to the workshop bench

Sanding drums used in a drill require one hand for the tool and the other to hold the piece being
sanded. Having the motor on the bench means both hands are free to hold the workpiece and offer it to
the sanding drum at various angles.

I have now made my own device, using an old washing machine motor. (You could, of course, use
a new ¼hp electric motor.) To this I fitted a three-jaw chuck which holds a 295mm (11⅝in) x 137mm
(5⅜in) diameter Sandboss pneumatic sanding drum, the largest currently available.

If you have to use a connector to fit the chuck to the motor shaft, make sure the thread and motor
direction do not cause the chuck to unthread in use.

I got a friend to tap on a new thread, which fitted my keyless chuck. This means I can quickly fit a
flexible shaft if required.

I find sanding star abrasive mops from CSM Trade Supplies of Brighton (Tel: 01273 600434) ideal
for smoothing curved areas. Using a range of grades increases the smoothness of the finished job.

Cliff Benton

POLISHING AID

Sometimes it can be difficult sanding or polishing in deep, inaccessible
areas of a carving with standard tools.

To help with this I use medical artery forceps, as used by surgeons.

I wrap a small piece of abrasive cloth round the end jaws of the forceps,
and this is held firmly in place by the locking mechanism on the handles,
which holds them together.

These forceps are invaluable for holding small pieces of wire wool and
Webrax pad or cloth for polishing.

The forceps are available with either straight or curved jaws and in a
wide variety of sizes. You can buy them from tool suppliers and fishing
tackle shops.

Dick Baugh

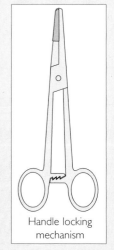

Handle locking
mechanism

Forceps with abrasive cloth wrapped round the jaws and locked in position

SURE SANDING

Sanding is perhaps the most tedious and time-consuming part of carving, particularly if the design is complex and difficult to access.

I use the following technique, which was shown me by a woodcarver in Toowoomba, Australia, many years ago.

First, cut a sheet of sandpaper into nine strips, each about 280 x 25mm (11 x 1in). You can cut two or three sheets together, using a steel rule and knife. I use a disposable knife with snap-off blades, as the abrasive soon blunts the cutting edge.

Take a strip and hold it between the thumb and first finger of your right hand (or left if you are left-handed). Place the ball of your left thumb on the strip as close as convenient to the end being held, pressing it against the area of wood to be sanded.

Now the tricky part. While pulling the strip of paper with your right hand under the pad of your left thumb, slowly move the left thumb in the direction the paper is being pulled.

When the whole length of paper has passed, the left thumb will have moved between 12 and 60mm (½ to 2⅜in) depending on the situation. The movement creates a shallow trench, which tends to remove the high spots first, allowing much greater control of the sanding. If you do not move your thumb, a small pit will be created in the wood

This technique works well in tight spots, provided your thumb, or even a finger, can access them. In such a situation make the strips narrower, and exert only light pressure with the left thumb.

The strips can be reversed for extra wear, but should be replaced after between 20 and 50 strokes.

I start with 120 grit because the backing paper is much thinner than that used on coarser grits. A good sequence is 120 grit for shaping, 240 grit for fine shaping and removal of most defects, 400 grit for find sanding and 600 grit wet and dry for a lovely satin finish.

On larger areas you can use the fingers of your left hand to form the pad rather than your thumb.

Beware the edge of the strip, as it can cut like a razor, so keep your left hand out of the way.

Extended use of this technique can wear your skin, so use a soft sticking plaster on the ball of each thumb and the side of your first finger for protection.

John Beasley

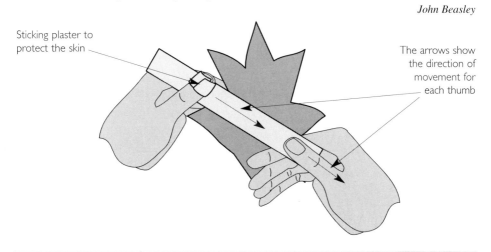

Sticking plaster to protect the skin

The arrows show the direction of movement for each thumb

Preparing and decorating wood

TOUGH TEETH

Here's an idea for adding realistic-looking teeth to wild animal carvings.

When I carved a dragon I used thorns of various lengths gathered from a rose bush. I left them to dry for a few days, then glued them into the dragon's mouth using epoxy resin (you could also use superglue). I held them in place with tweezers until the glue set.

The effect is realistic and lifelike and could be used for bears, lions, tigers, alligators and so on. You could also use thorns for birds' talons.

If rose thorns are too large, you could also use bramble thorns. Start with the smallest thorns at the back of each side of the mouth and use progressively larger ones as you get to the front teeth.

I painted the thorns white, but you could use varnish or stain.

G Mateer

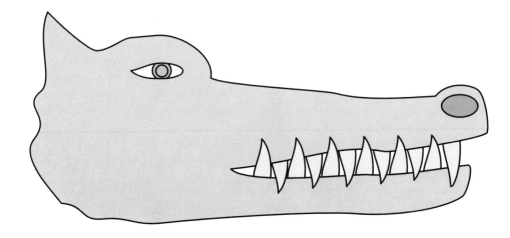

Thorns make great dragon teeth

DENT REPAIR

Here's a tip for removing a small dent on bare wood, which is too small to fill with wood filler.

Dents are caused by fibres in the wood being compacted under pressure. They can often be steamed out.

To do this, place a wet kitchen towel over the damage and go over it several times with a hot clothes iron. The steam will swell the fibres, which should then pop back into place.

Liberon

KEEP FIGURING

When carving light coloured woods such as lime (*Tilia vulgaris*) or sycamore (*Acer pseudoplatanus*), it is often difficult to maintain any clear, delicate figuring that may be present in the grain.

Some use sanding sealer or lacquer rubbed down with 0000 wire wool, but this can result in a grey bloom over the wood.

I use a dry fine Scotchbrite scouring pad instead, and this leaves no bloom or scratches. I do this whether I am using a sealer or not, often in place of sanding.

There is something to be said for using a white wax directly on the bare wood without any sealer. This will prevent any darkening of the wood and maintains the natural colour almost exactly.

It takes a bit more time to get a shine, but it is well worth the effort.

Peter Benson

COLOURING WOOD

For carving in miniature there is nothing to compare with a good piece of boxwood (B*uxus sempervirens*). It is not too difficult to obtain, and although it is hard, it is a pleasure to carve.

You can cut along or across the grain equally well and produce the most intricate, detailed work. The only disadvantage is that very often it has little figured grain, and it does not take wood stain too well.

Many musical instrument makers darken boxwood parts by fuming them with vapour of nitric acid, which can make it almost jet black.

A more suitable and safer method for us ordinary mortals is to dye the wood the colour we require, using Dylon fabric dyes. These have to be mixed with water and boiled. The carving is immersed for only 40 to 50 seconds, then removed and washed under the cold tap.

Pat it dry with a cloth and then leave it to dry thoroughly away from heat.

If areas of the carving are to be left uncoloured, they can be masked with latex or Copydex before immersion. This can easily be peeled off when dry. The results of this process are quite striking as contrasting colours are clearly defined with positive, clear lines.

I once saw a black stained netsuke of a chimpanzee with the face, palms and fingernails left the normal colour of the wood. The effect was amazing.

Peter Benson

N.B. Always take precautions when handling chemicals, especially acids.

KNOTTY SOLUTION

I carve birds and animals from logs, mostly yew (*Taxus baccata*), which I collect and season myself. I finish the carvings with pale French polish to show the grain.

Using logs often results in splits or holes caused by rotten wood appearing in the finished carving just where I do not want them.

You can use various colours of plastic wood or other stoppings for small cracks, but they stand out like a sore thumb on larger faults.

Large splits or holes need to be filled with wood of a similar colour to the surrounding area, but it is almost impossible to match the pattern of the grain, so large inserts are obvious.

I have found the best way to disguise inserts is to turn them into knots by copying an existing knot using plastic wood and wood stains. If this is done well, the result can be almost undetectable.

I keep a supply of seasoned sticks and branches suitable for filling large holes. These make instant knots complete with growth rings.

Geoff Morgan

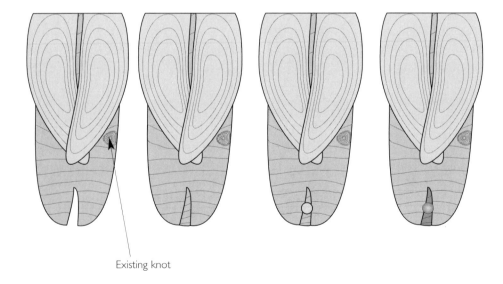

Existing knot

| Bird carving with a split in the tail | Wooden insert glued in | A hole is drilled and a plug glued in | Plastic wood varies the colour of the knot, then add stain |

BETTER BIRD HEADS

Fitting the head of a carved decoy bird to its body requires a perfect fit if the glue line is not to be seen.

Competition judges usually look most carefully at the head, so anything which improves its appearance will pay off, especially if your carving is not to be painted.

I find it almost impossible to get a perfect fit if I use a dowel to join the parts, as is often recommended. Instead, when bandsawing out the blanks, keep the base of the bird, the neck joint and the top of the head flat and parallel. They will of course be shaped later.

Now glue the head to the body and apply pressure using a drill press, or pillar drill, as a clamp. Use a suction cup or padding to spread the pressure on top of the bird's head.

Use a couple of brads with their heads cut off between the body and head to prevent slippage. If all three surfaces (the top of the head, the neck joint and the base of the bird) are not perfectly flat, you can use shims under the bird to make sure the pressure is distributed evenly.

When carving some birds, such as Canada geese or redheads, you can use contrasting woods to capitalise on the head/body join.

For Canada geese I use American black walnut (*Juglans nigra*) for the head and neck with an insert of maple (*Acer spp*) for the throat, and butternut (*Juglans cinera*) for the body.

W H Brown

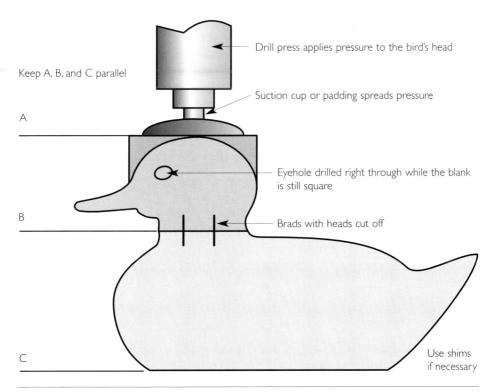

Keep A, B, and C parallel

Drill press applies pressure to the bird's head

Suction cup or padding spreads pressure

A

Eyehole drilled right through while the blank is still square

B

Brads with heads cut off

Use shims if necessary

C

Working hard wood

Some dense woods like walnut (*Juglans spp*) and yew (*Taxus baccata*) can be slow and wearying to carve.

Soften the wood by wrapping it in a damp cloth, leaving it outside in the rain, or even putting it in a bucket of water before working on it.

It will come to no harm but will be much easier to carve.

Sometimes elm (*Ulmus spp*) and the sap wood of walnut can be sticky to carve and you have to pull the gouge out after each cut.

This can be eased by scrubbing the surface you are about to carve with lukewarm water.

Zoë Gertner

Seasoning help

After some trial and much error I have found the best way of seasoning timber.

The timber should be from winter fellings when the sap is down. Cut it to sizes you will need for future carvings, as this reduces internal stress and speeds drying. Large logs are best stored as half or quarter sections.

Immediately seal sawn ends with Cuprinol No More Damp bitumen waterproofer. This is a thick bitumen emulsion, which can be thinned with water. Unlike wax or oil–based paint, it is compatible with wet wood, and dries quickly.

After a second coat the next day the black ends are ideal for recording the wood type and date with white paint.

If the bark is not loose or diseased, leave it undisturbed, but bark-free surfaces and section sides should be given a thin coat of sealant.

Store the sealed timber on deal offcut spacers in a drying shed. Mine is a simple structure attached to the back of the garage, made from larch lap fencing panels with a chipboard and felt roof.

The shed sits on several bricks, giving a 63mm (2½in) floor gap. This, with the loose structure of the fencing panels, allows good ventilation.

It is important not to fill the shed with garden clutter which would restrict free air movement.

I examine the stored wood when there are major changes of climate and, if there are signs of splits, I cover them with thick sealant.

The wood is ready for carving after allowing about one year per 25mm (1in) of thickness.

This time can be reduced by removing the sealant and using a microwave oven to complete seasoning.

Mike Norris

MIXING PAINTS

As a novice carver of birds and animals, I find it useful when carving patterns include the approximate colour mixes for the various areas to be painted. For example, 80% burnt umber, 10% raw umber, 5% ultramarine, and so on.

My problem was that I found it difficult to estimate these small relative amounts of paint, and my final mixes were often very different from those desired.

I have now developed a method of measuring more accurately.

Using a compass, I draw a series of circles on non–absorbent cardboard, the type with the shiny waxed surface sheen. The diameters of the circles are in proportion to the relative amounts of the colours to be mixed.

I then carefully dispense a blob of paint on to the appropriate circle and press it down gently to fill the area of the marked circle. I repeat the process for each colour, pressing gently to get the same thickness of paint blob.

Then I scrape the paint blobs off with a palette knife and mix them together on a white tile.

This technique has significantly improved my colour matches.

Gerry Sanger

AVOID BREAKAGE

Many carvers use basswood (*Tilia Americana*) or white pine (*Pinus strobus*) because they are soft timbers and easy to carve. However, if you undercut thin areas it can invite breakage or splitting.

Mack Sutter, who wrote two books and several articles on carving relief floral patterns, worked out a technique he called stabilising for protecting thin carved petals, leaves and stems.

This involved coating surfaces to be carved with a penetrating mixture to enable the wood to resist stresses. He tried a number of mixtures and found a 50-50 mix of denatured alcohol and shellac worked best.

You simply paint the mixture over complex areas and allow it to dry before you start carving. Repeat the process as carving progresses beyond the effective depth of penetration of the stabiliser.

I suggested he use a harder wood, but that would have involved using a mallet, which he did not like.

The stabiliser leaves a shellac shine on the wood, but this can be dulled down by washing with neat denatured alcohol.

E J Tangerman

Wood saver

If you have an irregular or wedge-shaped block of wood and want to get the maximum size carving from it, do not remove wood to square it up. Instead add scrap wood to square it up. This will enable you to mark out the design and cut it out safely on the bandsaw.

First, mentally position your carving within the chosen block and trim off any damaged or projecting pieces, such as ragged edges and corners.

Stand the block on a piece of paper, draw round it and enclose with a close fitting rectangle. This will show where scrap wood has to be added.

Where you need to add scrap along the full length, to ensure a sound joint, the surface should be planed flat. The flats do not need to be parallel to the centre and may taper.

Glue scrap wood, also with a flat surface, in place, using wood filler if necessary. Nail and clamp the strips in place.

When the glue has set, remove the nails and shape the scrap with a handsaw, plane or file, until you have a rectangular block.

Now you can draw on your shape and cut it out on the bandsaw. Any scraps still glued to the corners will probably be carved away when you rough out.

The illustrations show how I was able to get the largest possible sized cat from a wedge of walnut (*Juglans spp*) using the narrow end for the head.

This minimises wastage of expensive timber and avoids risks with the bandsaw.

John Beart

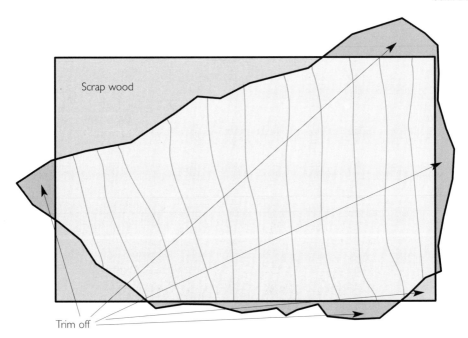

This wedge needs just two pieces of scrap glued on

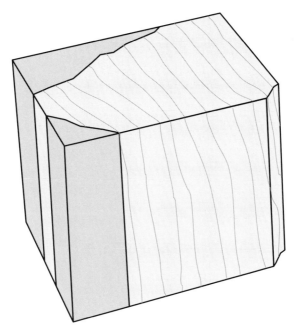

Walnut block with scraps added to square it up

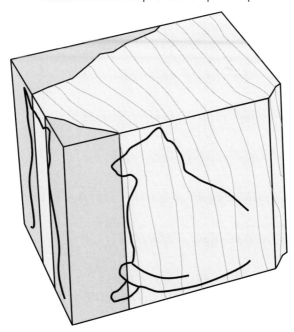

Outline of a cat drawn on ready for bandsawing. The scrap wood will be removed when roughing out

HOME-MADE PUNCHES

If you want repeated small holes or dents in a carving, for example to represent seeds in a flower, you can achieve this quickly by making random indentations using a brad or nail with a small hammer.

For a more regular pattern, grind or file the end of a large nail flat, then cross-hatch it with a triangular file to make a punch which will make several dots with each blow.

For larger patterns, the nail head itself can be patterned.

Professional carvers, who make birds and animals, use punches for the eyes.

Shape punches from a rod or spike with a hand grinder, so it will indent a rim and leave a central mound.

E J Tangerman

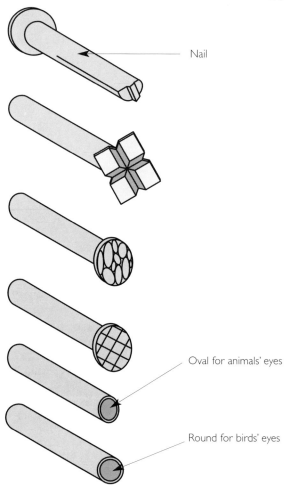

Nail

Oval for animals' eyes

Round for birds' eyes

Examples of home-made punches

GOOD PUPILS

There are lots of books and articles on carving eyes, but few give advice on sizing and carving the pupils.

The size can have a big influence on the expression you wish to convey, and the direction of sight, and a small error in position can produce a cross–eyed effect. Perhaps this is why eyes are sometimes left without pupils.

When marking pupils it is best not to draw them on as this can be messy if you want to change them.

Instead, use black PVC insulation tape, available from electrical or hardware shops. Cut out two circular pupils in the required size, using scissors or a suitably-sized gouge. Place them on the eyes, move them about until they are in the right position and then stick them on firmly. They can be trimmed at the top to move them under the eyelid, and other sizes tried until you get the effect you want.

Finally, draw carefully around the tape pupil with a fine pencil, or better still cut around with the same gouge used to cut them out, and then finish carving the pupil.

John Beart

FASTER FUR

Carving animal fur can be incredibly time-consuming and boring. A fast alternative, which works on many woods with a fine, even texture, is to use a tungsten carbide burr.

Stroke a coarse burr over the wood, going in the direction of the fur, then sand lightly with a very fine abrasive paper wrapped around a soft block or your fingers. This will produce a tactile feel, which appears to have been laboriously carved with a scalpel.

Varying the burr, the speed, the rate of feed or the wood changes the results, producing spines, thatch and so on.

Rod Naylor

Index

D

dents, removing 56
depth cutting jigs, making 8
die grinders
    suspended from ceiling for easier use 9
    used in place of flexible shaft tools 8
drawings
    holders for, made from music stands 4
    shading, as an aid to visualising
      carving 33
drawknives, made from hacksaw blades 15
dust-extraction systems, home-made 52
dyeing wood 57

E

electric drills, used to rough out large
    blocks 28
engraving machines, suspended from
    ceiling for easier use 8
eyes in carvings, positioning 65

F

fans, carving 29
files, cleaning in water 4
firmers, made from hacksaw blades 16
flexible shaft tools, substitutes for 8
fuming wood 57
fur for animal carvings, quickly
    rendered with burrs 65

G

glue
    hiding glue lines in laminated
      blocks 29
    storing in shower gel bottles 6
gouges
    controlling radius of cut 20
    grinding inside for greater control 20
    made from hacksaw blades 16
    making templates of profiles 11
grinding edge tools 20–2, 24

H

hacksaw blades, adapted as tools 15–16

hand tools
    depth cutting jigs for 8
    grinding and stropping 20–2
    holding like a pencil for
      control 12, 31
    jigs for sharpening 24
    made from hacksaw blades 15–16
    power tool burrs, used as 25
    see also chisels, drawknives, firmers,
    gouges, micro scorps, punches,
    scrapers, tool handles, V tools
honing strops, making 22
hot air paint strippers, used to
    straighten walking sticks 26

I

ice-cream containers, used as tool
    holders 4

K

kebab sticks, used to joint small pieces 32
knots, used to disguise blemishes in
    wood 58

L

laminated blocks, hiding glue lines in 29
lead-weighted mallets, making 9
leather
    belts, used as tool carrying case 4
    honing strops, making 22
lettering, carved, painting 32
limewood, bringing out the grain in 57
lolly sticks, adapted as sanding sticks 53

M

mallets
    heavy, making 9
    palm, made from rubber mallets 18
micro scorps, making 23
mirrors
    car, adaped as workholders 48
    used to position mitres 28
mitres, positioning with a mirror 28
music stands, used as drawings holders 4

WOODCARVING

The Art of the Woodcarver	*GMC Publications*
Carving Birds & Beasts	*GMC Publications*
Carving on Turning	*Chris Pye*
Carving Realistic Birds	*David Tippey*
Decorative Woodcarving	*Jeremy Williams*
Essential Tips for Woodcarvers	*GMC Publications*
Essential Woodcarving Techniques	*Dick Onians*
Further Useful Tips for Woodcarvers	*GMC Publications*
Lettercarving in Wood: A Practical Course	*Chris Pye*
Power Tools for Woodcarving	*David Tippey*
Practical Tips for Turners & Carvers	*GMC Publications*
Relief Carving in Wood: A Practical Introduction	*Chris Pye*
Understanding Woodcarving	*GMC Publications*
Understanding Woodcarving in the Round	*GMC Publications*
Useful Techniques for Woodcarvers	*GMC Publications*
Wildfowl Carving – Volume 1	*Jim Pearce*
Wildfowl Carving – Volume 2	*Jim Pearce*
The Woodcarvers	*GMC Publications*
Woodcarving: A Complete Course	*Ron Butterfield*
Woodcarving: A Foundation Course	*Zoe Gertner*
Woodcarving for Beginners	*GMC Publications*
Woodcarving Tools & Equipment Test Reports	*GMC Publications*
Woodcarving Tools, Materials & Equipment	*Chris Pye*

WOODTURNING

Adventures in Woodturning	*David Springett*
Bert Marsh: Woodturner	*Bert Marsh*
Bill Jones' Notes from the Turning Shop	*Bill Jones*
Bill Jones' Further Notes from the Turning Shop	*Bill Jones*
Bowl Turning Techniques Masterclass	*Tony Boase*
Colouring Techniques for Woodturners	*Jan Sanders*
The Craftsman Woodturner	*Peter Child*
Decorative Techniques for Woodturners	*Hilary Bowen*
Faceplate Turning	*GMC Publications*
Fun at the Lathe	*R.C. Bell*
Further Useful Tips for Woodturners	*GMC Publications*
Illustrated Woodturning Techniques	*John Hunnex*
Intermediate Woodturning Projects	*GMC Publications*
Keith Rowley's Woodturning Projects	*Keith Rowley*
Multi-Centre Woodturning	*Ray Hopper*
Practical Tips for Turners & Carvers	*GMC Publications*
Practical Tips for Woodturners	*GMC Publications*
Spindle Turning	*GMC Publications*
Turning Green Wood	*Michael O'Donnell*

WOODWORKING

TOYMAKING

Designing & Making Wooden Toys	*Terry Kelly*
Fun to Make Wooden Toys & Games	*Jeff & Jennie Loader*
Making Wooden Toys & Games	*Jeff & Jennie Loader*
Restoring Rocking Horses	*Clive Green & Anthony Dew*
Scrollsaw Toy Projects	*Ivor Carlyle*
Scrollsaw Toys for All Ages	*Ivor Carlyle*
Wooden Toy Projects	*GMC Publications*

VIDEOS

Elliptical Turning	*David Springett*
Woodturning Wizardry	*David Springett*
Turning Between Centres: The Basics	*Dennis White*
Turning Bowls	*Dennis White*
Boxes, Goblets and Screw Threads	*Dennis White*
Novelties and Projects	*Dennis White*
Classic Profiles	*Dennis White*
Twists and Advanced Turning	*Dennis White*
Sharpening the Professional Way	*Jim Kingshott*
Sharpening Turning & Carving Tools	*Jim Kingshott*
Bowl Turning	*John Jordan*
Hollow Turning	*John Jordan*
Woodturning: A Foundation Course	*Keith Rowley*
Carving a Figure: The Female Form	*Ray Gonzalez*

MAGAZINES

WOODTURNING ♦ WOODCARVING ♦ FURNITURE & CABINETMAKING

THE DOLLS' HOUSE MAGAZINE ♦ THE ROUTER ♦ THE SCROLLSAW

BUSINESSMATTERS ♦ WATER GARDENING

The above represents a selection of the titles currently published or scheduled to be published.
All are available direct from the Publishers or through bookshops, newsagents and specialist retailers.
To place an order, or to obtain a complete catalogue, contact:

GMC Publications,
Castle Place, 166 High Street, Lewes, East Sussex BN7 1XU, United Kingdom
Tel: 01273 488005 Fax: 01273 478606

Orders by credit card are accepted